The South
and
Christian Ethics

JAMES SELLERS

The South
and
Christian Ethics

ASSOCIATION PRESS   NEW YORK

THE SOUTH AND CHRISTIAN ETHICS

Copyright © 1962 by

National Board of Young Men's Christian Associations

Association Press, 291 Broadway, New York 7, N.Y.

All rights reserved, including the right of reproduction
in whole or in part in any form, under the International,
Pan-American, and Universal Copyright Conventions.

Publisher's Stock Number: 1502

Library of Congress catalog card number: 62-16877

72

Printed in the United States of America

To my colleagues

of the Vanderbilt Divinity School faculty

who gave to the making

of this book

Preface

I HAVE attempted in this book to reflect, as a Southerner and as a teacher of Christian ethics, on the meaning of today's racial conflict in the South. My aim has been to say something helpful about a single question: how may men of the next generation become better neighbors? This problem, of course, transcends the South and is a national and even global one; and it involves various conflicts other than the encounter between white and Negro. Yet I see the need for working on it in a concrete situation, and I believe that the South is now becoming a testing ground or pilot area where this deepest challenge of our times—the challenge to live together—can be approached constructively by men of good will.

That is why I begin, after an introductory chapter, with an examination of the South and its way, and why, all through the book, I have given over much space to the mind sets and the frailties and the auguries of promise among various sorts of Southerners.

Some readers will doubtless feel, when they have finished, that I have paid too much, or too little, attention to the white Southerner, or that I have favored or slighted or failed to understand the Negro Southerner. I freely concede my limitations. In a book of this kind a writer has to fall back, inevitably, on what he knows of himself —and for himself. John Howard Griffin has reminded us in his recent report, *Black Like Me*, for example, just how hard it is for a white man, even one who casts his lot with the Negro and passes for a Negro, to get inside and fathom the Negro. I have done the best I can, but I have no special clairvoyance.

There is another enigma that I have attempted to ponder. This is the mind of the reticent Southern white. Those of us who participate willingly in the transformation of human ways now afoot in the South find it difficult to close with those, even of our homeplaces, who seem so taken aback that changes must come. Again, I have tried.

What does it mean to insist we should be thinking out how these Southerners may now become neighbors?

It means we face a shift of eras. Segregation is a sick, dying way of life. Hard battles are yet to be fought, but the white supremacist is going to lose. Yet the result is often to leave the races in contemptuous estrangement. Christians cannot be content with such an outcome; they must work for some kind of fellowship between white and Negro in the uncharted territory beyond desegregation.

One way to proceed is to resist seeing Southerners in tired old ways. We must no longer look upon the white simply as someone out of whom concessions must be exacted. He is a human being in need of fellowship and the kind of understanding that redeems, for after he has been made to swallow the bitter pill of undoing his segregated world, he will still be there. Similarly, we must resist seeing the Negro simply as someone for whom concessions must be wrested. It is now no longer proper (if it ever was) to view the Negro as the hapless stranger in the land who does not quite know how to keep out of the path of evil masters. He has shown us the growing irrelevance of this stereotype by asserting his manhood convincingly over the past few years.

And what does the word "neighbor" mean as we use it here? Some will be reminded of the geographical sense. Today the Negro is a very much suppressed neighbor in that sense, for he has been penned up, denied living space. This situation clamors for attention, but the word "neighbor" as it occurs in this book nearly always has a broader meaning. When I say white and Negro must now become better neighbors, I mean, quite simply, that we must learn on both sides how to treat each other as human beings. Let us not confuse what I am asking—human encounter—with a counterfeit sentimentality. If segregation will no longer work, if justice steeped in hostility is not a solution, neither will artificial togetherness produce neighbors. What can create neighbors, though, is to learn to respect and live with each other as men. How we may make a start in the South, remembering that "nothing . . . is a greater absurdity, than a morose, hard, close, high-spirited, spiteful true Christian" (Jonathan Edwards) is the subject of this book.

For the counsel and help they have given me (not always knowing it), I am grateful to the following friends, who should be exonerated, of course, from all responsibility for the defects of this study: Will D. Campbell, James D. Glasse, Vincent and Rosemarie Harding, Gordon D. Kaufman, John D. Maguire, Richard H. Rice, Lou H. Silberman. I am also indebted to participants in the regional conference of the Methodist Student Movement held at Atlanta in November, 1961, for critical discussions of some of the ideas of this volume, which were presented as lectures there.

JAMES SELLERS

Vanderbilt University

Contents

CHAPTER 1

The Crucial Issue

The Negro has lost some of his former virtues and a good many illusions. Gone is his celebrated patience, his childlike obedience, and his colossal fear. He has waited 98 years. . . . The day he stopped being a good old Negro was the day he became a man.

—EBONY [1]

The Crucial Issue

IT IS very likely that the people I grew up with in the panhandle of West Florida will take a dim view of me for beginning with a quotation from *Ebony* magazine. (In case your sense of geography fails you, the Florida panhandle is much closer to Dothan, Alabama, and Lucedale, Mississippi, and Thomasville, Georgia, than it is to Miami; in fact, the Alabama legislature tried to annex us one time.) And yet I claim to be different from them in only one way. I am neither a better Christian than they are, for we are all sinners, nor a poorer Southerner, for Yankees sometimes irk me, too. I do claim to be more realistic, I suppose. I begin with *Ebony* because I think this statement provides us with the key to the crucial ethical issue facing Americans at home today.

What is this issue? It may be simply put, though it touches the quick of American life: *can we live together as men?* Up to now, where the Negro is concerned, we have found ways to avoid the question. We have co-existed with the Negro, but we have not *lived* with him, for that means recognizing his manhood. Today the Negro revolt of the 1950's and 1960's has forced upon us what Louis E. Lomax calls "the incredible truth of the Negro." It is a truth that even the "white liberal" is hard-pressed to understand, for it requires seeing the Negro as what he is, not as what his detractors or even his well-meaning friends have thought he was—or should be.

I would question only one part of *Ebony's* comment, and that is the suggestion that the Negro "has waited 98 years." That is true, in a way, of course. But it is not quite the full truth. The Negro "stopped being a good old Negro" and "became a man" only a few short years ago. For not until after World War II did he really begin to see himself as a man and to *act* as such; before, he had all too often gone along with the white man in agreeing to a secondary, segregated status within our society. He did so mostly because he had to, perhaps, but he did so. More-over, the churches, white and Negro alike, even the prophets of the far-famed Social Gospel, were until recently quite willing to leave the Negro, for all practical purposes, to his role of second-class citizen. Certainly the courts of our land, from 1896 onward for two generations or so, pegged the Negro's humanity at less than parity through the "separate but equal" fiction.

If the Negro has been waiting these ten decades, then, he has been waiting, in part, on himself, and in part on some of those forces now enrolled so vigorously on his behalf.

The U.S. Supreme Court's 1954 decision against segregated schools was one of a long series of milestones leading up to an explosive transition. (Actually, the legal shortcomings of the "separate but equal" theory were beginning to be exposed as early as 1938, when the Supreme Court required a state to take the theory seriously and in fact furnish equal facilities.[2]) But the transition itself came even later. The "new Negro" we are so much aware of today found himself, I believe, as late as December 5, 1955, when the boycott of segregated buses in Montgomery, Alabama, began. But once the Negro did find himself, the foot dragging of white Southerners and other Americans unready to accept him didn't turn out to be so fatal, after all.

To be sure, long before the sit-in era, there were Negro leaders—W. E. B. DuBois is a classic example, but only one name out of a host we could list—who insisted on full rights and equality for their fellows. How could it be, then, that the "new Negro" was so late in realizing himself? Before the sit-in era, vital ingredients were still lacking. Not the will to justice: the National Association for the Advancement of Colored People has been going since 1910. At least some sectors of the Negro community have long since been wealthy, as anyone who has lived in Atlanta or Birmingham well knows. And the slaves had hardly been set free before a cadre of educated, productive Negro scientists and teachers began to emerge.

One thing lacking until recently was a broad distribution of these capacities—the "critical mass" that permits the chain reaction of a leap to freedom. In the whole of the nineteenth century, fewer than 2,500 Negroes were graduated from American colleges. As late as 1930, no more than 27,000 Negroes were enrolled in our colleges. By contrast, in 1960 there were upwards of 200,000.[3] Thus to the deep, seething resentments and the thirst for manhood that may have been at work beneath the surface for decades, the Negro has recently added the ability to act for himself in numbers, convincingly and permanently.

An even more important missing ingredient was the confidence of Christian decision that enables the young of a people to grasp its material and cultural blessings and put them to the service of declaring its manhood. The sociologist E. Franklin Frazier tells us in his *Black Bourgeoisie* about the old fears of affluent, middle-class Negroes, fears that have restrained them from asserting any genuine selfhood on a par with whites. Even with their economic power, then, they agreed to a segregated society that sheltered them from reality. Indeed, segregation continues even now to pay off for many of them financially.

Beginning with the sit-in generation, the Negro has at last broken through the ring of such fears, has learned to place freedom, with all its risks, above the certainty of creature comforts; he has called the white man's bluff.

So I would disagree mildly with *Ebony*. The white man hasn't exactly been suppressing the *new* Negro for 98 years, because there hasn't been a "new Negro" that long. The whole picture of what it means to be a Negro in America has just dawned on us.

"Look at their methods, though," white friends in the South tell me. "Some are lawbreakers. All are bent on driving the races further apart." Noting the frequent violation of local segregation laws as a method of protest, these friends insist that "racial progress must be based on obedience to the law."

All right, the methods of the "new Negroes" *are* sometimes dangerous. To be sure, we ought to look upon law and action through the courts as the fundamental manner in our country of securing justice and change. Moreover, the "new Negroes" have not succeeded in creating instantly what they talk about a lot (talk about too much just yet, perhaps): *community*. But let us remember: there's no genuine community except between free men. And the only way for a man to become a man may be to cut himself off for the time being from the community that still regards him as a child. His methods inevitably are going to shake those already in seats of authority. Let us remember, further, that some of the most respected Christian leaders in our land have reluctantly decided that those few laws still left standing that require racial discrimination may be such serious violations of our sense of justice as to make peaceable and orderly protest of them, even disobedience of them by nonviolent means, entirely respectable.

Contrary to mythology propagated by elements of both races, a surprising number of white Southerners welcome these developments as the lifting of a burden. Let us listen to James McBride Dabbs, Calvinist elder, South Carolinian, plantation owner, grandson of a Confederate warrior:

> . . . The desire for justice among both Negroes and white is growing strong in the South. . . . The fact remains that we are more concerned than our fathers were how to live together in the world. It may be because it is becoming more difficult to live together in the world. . . . Perhaps we have built, all unintentionally, a world which demands that we follow more closely the Judaeo-Christian tradition.[4]

To fight the segregation battle longer is, for Dabbs, to live in the past, to fret with the wrong problem. The problem now, and it does not concern American whites and Negroes alone, is "how to live together in the world." Such talk brings a flood of abuse from racists in this second half of the enlightened twentieth century. But such Southerners as Dabbs and the late novelist William Faulkner were willing to absorb it. "We accept insult and contumely and the risk of violence," Faulkner said, "because we will not sit quietly by and see our native land, the South, . . . wreck and ruin itself twice in less than a hundred years"—over the wrong question.

Planetary, Yet Close to Home

The real question before us, Faulkner goes on, is not "white against black." That is a pseudo-question. The question is whether we want to remain free people. Soon we shall have to make a choice about that. "We will have to chose not between color nor race nor religion," he says, "but simply between being slaves and being free." It is a choice we shall have to make completely, for we can't have a little bit of each. You can't have a freedom that you don't practice, you can't expect to keep a right that you won't grant. People who want to be free, Faulkner says, had better stick together; what matters is not whether they are "black people nor white people nor pink nor blue nor green people," but rather that they are people who want to be free.[5]

That just about sums it up, I think. Dabbs calls the problem the one of "how to live together in the world." Faulkner calls it the choice before us of accepting others who want to be free, or else of all falling into some kind of "slavedom" while we concern ourselves with a false color problem. Take it either way. What starts simply as the "Negro question" turns out to be but a part of the whole vast and fearful issue of how men shall live with other men. It is man's problem in all ages, but it is America's problem in a particularly terrifying age.

The problem before us in America and the South, then, is not too different from the international questions that claim so much of our horror-stricken attention today. It is not separated from the problem of world peace, or of what to do about communism, or of the rapidly rising nonwhite peoples of Asia and Africa, or of nuclear fission.

Moreover, history suggests that the "new Negro's" revolutionary methods are not so novel, after all. No rising people yet has won its freedom in calm, orderly debate. We have only to look at our own American struggle for independence. British rule was legal and orderly, from the point of view of the British. Our own national revolt had to follow an unsmooth path and risk the upsetting of calm that inevitably goes into a people's emergence upon freedom.

The same thing is happening all over the world today. Only the revolts are faster-paced than before. Most Europeans and all Americans know freedom that has been won in a series of revolutions stretching over four centuries or so; these newer peoples—partly because of our methods of colonizing—are having to emerge in one or two short generations. European Protestants, for example, have had nearly five hundred years to absorb the impact of what it means to be free as a Christian; the Reformation is that old. Americans have had nearly two hundred years to get used to freedom from empire, and to experiment with what were, in 1776, novel political rights. All of us in the Western world have had even a little longer than that to learn how to make the most of our reason, rediscovered in the intellectual upheavals of the Enlightenment. Finally, we in America are just now barely beginning to handle ourselves responsibly in the industrial and labor fields, for here, too, we have undergone

22

a revolution that has given us bread and leisure and added depth to our freedom.[6]

Partly because of the speed with which we have exported Western civilization, all these revolutions have come at once upon the newer peoples of Asia and Africa. Is it any wonder that their emergence has been attended by disorder and sometimes by tragedy? It is little help to declaim piously, "They should have waited." The impulse to freedom can no more be stored, mellowed, and aged than can lightning bolts. Besides, one group of men hardly has a perpetual right to set the timetable for the freedom of other men. That is only a subtle denial of freedom itself. Some will take the plunge too soon, no doubt, from our comfortable American point of view. But the remedy is not to try to make dependents of them again. Our duty, rather, is to understand that they are men struggling themselves to hold aloft the heavy, gangling banner of freedom. If we do not help them, the "slave-dom" Faulkner speaks of is there waiting for them—and then, perhaps, for us, too.

Before us, then, is the very question, if you want to be pragmatic, of America's survival. And if you also want to look at the question ethically, it is the central New Testament mystery of how we shall treat our neighbors. Next only to how we respond to God it is the most pressing concern men can face; and really it is not different, finally, from the question of how we respond to God, seeing that Jesus links the two together as one (Matthew 22:39).

Where Do We Go from Here?

A generation ago, the central ethical problems faced by Americans revolved around the working man's place in a rich industrial society. Today, as we have seen, our central concern has come to focus elsewhere. It is not now the problems of economic underprivilege or of the oppression of labor (favorite themes of the old Social Gospel) that transfix us. Indeed, we still have such problems. But a chief point of focus for Christian-ethical thought today is undoubtedly in race relations—the primary instance at home for us just now of the challenge of living together.

We can and must eliminate segregation in our schools and other public facilities, in businesses depending on general public patronage, and so on. On this point, I have to disagree, reluctantly, with those fellow Southerners, white and black, who in my opinion still live on in the past. On the other hand, there is a far deeper side of this problem, for desegregation of *everything* would in no sense of itself bring the kingdom of God to America or guarantee in the least what the New Testament means by neighborliness. At every level of progress, the self-oriented human heart finds new ways of rebelling against God and of shutting out other men. When the slaves were freed, that did not solve all problems, but only provided temptation for the evil of segregation to be installed. When segregation in the public places is eliminated, the evil of man's estrangement from man can and will continue in more refined ways. The question before

24

us is finally one of what goes on in men's hearts. This is just what cannot be managed or legislated.

My friends in a small West Florida town, a livestock-and-peanut center where I ran a weekly newspaper in palmier days, have told me in fairly militant terms that they will never accept integrated schools. I mention them not because they are unique, but rather because they are probably representative of the small-town South. Nevertheless, I do not believe them. I think they will accept integrated schools, and sooner than they suspect. In the first place, they are no more able finally to avoid the law of this land than were the people of Clinton, Tennessee, or of New Orleans. Both compulsion and conscience have a way of changing things. When the "new Negroes" get around to this town, the schools will become biracial or will close. ("Then they'll close," a friend remarked.) My friends there, if they will pardon me for saying so, are enjoying themselves on borrowed time; in a sense they are living off the sufferance of the Negro.

It is what will happen then and afterward in the hearts of the people of this town, and in the hearts of the Negroes, that really captures my attention. Desegregation is coming; that is not a debatable point any more. But working out an ethic of "men living together" means far more than devising the end of segregation. It means taking up the decidedly theological question of how men living in a hard and practical world may inwardly become neighbors. To fellow white Southerners, I have to insist that men cannot in the long run be neighbors over the high fence of segregation. To the victims of segregation and especially their patrons of neo-abolitionist illusions, I have to insist with equal force that removing the fence, after all, doesn't automatically make neighbors or solve the deepest problem. Equality and mutual access are prerequisites to neighborliness; this many Southerners and other Americans haven't seen. But equality and mutual access are only the external conditions for neighborliness; this, perhaps, most of us haven't seen.

The modern South, in my view, offers unusually suitable "living terrain" on which to think about and attack this deepest problem. And the intensity of the racial conflict in the South is only one of the reasons. Once we allow for its historic fixation on the specter of race, the South really has a great deal to contribute positively to the study of Christian ethics. Paradoxically, the South may be uniquely equipped to encourage democratic living, according to William H. Nicholls, an economist who is no friend of Southern traditionalism. Granting that there are problems, he says, yet "I found the South an unusually tolerant environment in which to live through the decade of anti-Communist hysteria in which McCarthy and his lesser lieutenants ... rode roughshod over civil rights." Today, the South, like other regions, has lent a certain support to John Birchery and other questionable expressions of a valid anti-Communist feeling. But Nicholls' observation probably still holds: "From this experience I was convinced that, the race issue aside, the South could evince the widest and most genuine support for basic civil rights of all American regions." [7]

Beyond this receptivity to democratic standards, however, the South as a region has much to contribute directly to the crucial issue of how to live with other men as neighbors. Has our machine age taken some of the personal quality out of life? Maybe the South has resisted this trend a little more successfully than other regions. One of the vice presidents of the Southern Bell Telephone and Telegraph Company was complaining to a Nashville reporter recently. It seems that in the South, unlike some other sections, the people still insist on making their long-distance calls person to person instead of using the new, more efficient (but also more impersonal) direct dialing system.

"I don't know why," he remarked. "It seems to be a characteristic of the Southern people."

I can sympathize with the telephone company, but I would also point to the symbolic value of this Southern preference for the personal: to a very large extent, the South still holds out more promise than the North of teaching us what it means to have a home, to live amid change in a settled fashion, to make something enduring and personal and profound out of human associations.

Without suggesting that awakened Southerners are going to fetch the millennium for us, I think the South can now do two things toward realizing neighborliness for itself and the nation, and even the world. The first, as I have said, is to learn what it means to treat the Negro in all public contexts as a man. This part of the job will have to be carried out whether Southerners want to do it or not. The forms of justice and the very manhood of the Negro in his new life assure that. But the second thing is something that we can do only by decision and faith, and by accepting God's favor upon us, and that is to resolve, "beyond desegregation," to treat freshly the age-old problem of what it means for men to live as neighbors with other men. Our future depends on it.

The Rest of This Book

Before we go further, a hint of what is ahead may be helpful. As I have already suggested (see the preface), Chapter 2 is given over to a description of the Southerner's view of reality, at least as I see it. But the reader is entitled to have before him my understanding of what theology and Christian ethics have to say about our problem. So Chapter 3 provides a brief summary of the ethical and theological ideas that were in the back of my mind all along.

In the final two chapters, I have tried to put these things—attention to the South, and attention to Christian ethics—into constructive partnership. In Chapter 4 I have set out my view of what we can and should be doing about segregation. In Chapter 5 I have moved to the crucial problem, the question of what we ought to be doing above and beyond desegregation, to realize the challenge of "men living together."

Notes for Chapter 1

1. April, 1961, p. 88.
2. *Missouri ex rel. Gaines vs. Canada*, 305 U.S. 337 (1938).
3. Benjamin Muse, "A Virginia View of 'Race and Reason,'" *New South*, December, 1961, p. 15.

4. James McBride Dabbs, *The Southern Heritage* (New York: Alfred A. Knopf, Inc., 1959), pp. 248-249.
5. William Faulkner, "American Segregation and the World Crisis," *Three Views of the Segregation Decisions* (Atlanta: Southern Regional Council, 1956), pp. 10-12.
6. "Aufgaben und Möglichkeiten Christlichen Handelns im Raschen Sozialen Umbruch," *Zeitschrift für Evangelische Ethik*, September, 1960, pp. 257-318.
7. William H. Nicholls, *Southern Tradition and Regional Progress* (Chapel Hill: University of North Carolina Press, 1960), p. 140.

CHAPTER 2

The Two Kingdoms of God in America

> In their unique historic experience as Americans the Southerners should not only be able to find the basis for continuity of their heritage but also make contributions that balance and complement the experience of the rest of the nation.
>
> —C. VANN WOODWARD [1]

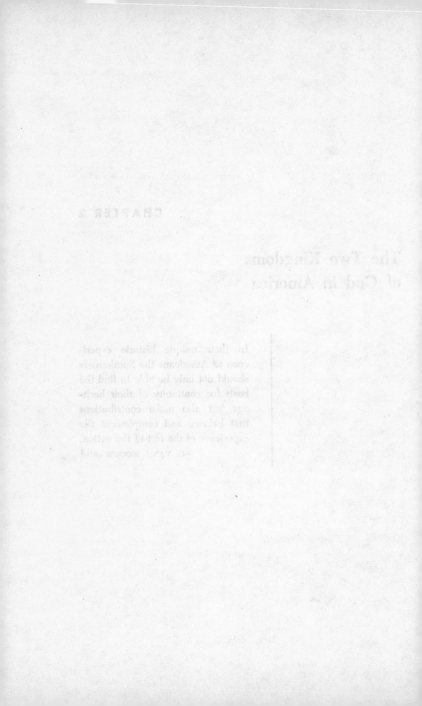

The Two Kingdoms
of God in America

TWO RECENT books of essays on the South's prospects, written by Southerners, take widely divergent views. The thesis of the one, *The Lasting South* (1957), is an "essential Southernness" about the South which permits this region to keep an identity of its own. "The South's identity is worth preserving," says the preface. Some contributors go further: one talks confidently about the "two civilizations of quite different impulse" that have grown up in the United States.

The thesis of the other, *The Southerner as American* (1960), moves the opposite way: its authors believe "that the traditional emphasis on the South's differentness and on the conflict between Southernism and Americanism is wrong historically." One of its contributors presses with insistence that "Americans Below the Potomac" are no different from other Americans culturally, never have been, and now that the "sole cause" of a separate point of view, slavery, has long since been eliminated, the South is proceeding to be reabsorbed into "the national society."

These two sets of authors, largely teachers in colleges and universities, are fitly seen as recent parties to a debate that has been going on for at least a century. One side maintains that North and South represent two distinct societies, or at least subcultures. The other typically holds, as we have seen, that the only important difference lay in slavery and its after-effects, and that therefore all traces of Southern separateness might well be searched out and discouraged.

Neither side is right; both sides are right. North and South *are* different, and in some quite important ways. But the differences are growing less, and they have never been so sharp as some traditionalists have claimed. "So slight a thing as a trip downtown on the bus may have in the South a ritual quality quite unintelligible to the Northern subway rider," Roger L. Shinn observes. That is not so spectacular a difference as the old myths could produce—myths which seemed to think of the South as populated by Cavaliers who ran plantations, studied the classics, and taught Hebrew to the slaves in the evenings; myths which had the North overrun with sweatshop proprietors and reformers with a tendency to migraine headaches. But these smaller differences of point of view and

34

habit—the special meaning of a bus trip to town in Raleigh or Baton Rouge are the very kind of difference that bears much significance for the ethicist or theologian. They are differences which, when added up, spell out a special view of the world, a special view of man's place in it, a special view of the world's Maker. They are differences which show up, finally, on the social scientist's scales, for they are differences which use land, money, time, and human relations as ways of finding an outlet.

However, let us not beg the embarrassing question. What about the racial issue—is *it* not, after all, the chief difference between North and South? We have good authority that it is. In a near-classic essay, Ulrich B. Phillips maintained in 1928 that the "central theme" of Southern history, and the basis of the region's differentness, is the white man's determination that the South "shall be and remain a white man's country." The idea can be put in various ways—in the crudities of a demagogue, or in the subtleties of a patrician. But whatever the form, it is always "the cardinal test of a Southerner and the central theme of Southern history." [2]

The theologian can take such claims seriously; he expects to find evidence of original sin, selfishness, and pride, whenever he looks deeply into the workings of a people. On the other hand, though he may agree that the thing to do is to urge elimination of white supremacy, he will yet pause to ask: what went wrong here? what special gift out of creation did the Southerner misuse to end up with this tragic situation of slavery and its aftermath?

Let us trace the Southerner's special view of the world

35

backward, to get at its roots. Given his tendency to white supremacy, we have to conclude one thing: he has *failed* at it. We may infer immediately, then, that a most important asset of the Southerner's world view is his knowledge of failure. We Southerners learned something from the Civil War and its hard corollary, Reconstruction, that most Americans have simply never had to bother with: what it means to be beaten, to be ground under and kept under, that it is possible, as Louis D. Rubin, Jr., says, "to do one's best and to lose." This element in the background of Southern thinking is more important, both in defining the distinctiveness of the South and in looking for a contribution the South can make to the nation, than we ordinarily recognize. The hollowness of the American cult of "success" is now coming generally to be assumed, and perhaps the day is not far off when Southerners can testify before Americans at large about something they, along with the European existentialists, have realized for a long time: a man may come to know himself more truly in defeat and failure than in abundant and easy success. As the historian Woodward puts it:

Generations of scarcity and want constitute one of the distinctive historical experiences of the Southern people, ... too deeply embedded in their memory to be wiped out by a business boom and too deep not to admit of some uneasiness at being characterized historically as a "People of Plenty." [3]

Thus, the Southern knowledge of defeat is not narrowly limited to military reversal. It includes not only a massive setback on the field of arms, but "long decades of defeat in the provinces of economic, social, and political life." Following World Wars I and II European voices have come forward striking the same note about the degree of reality which may be seen in one's crises. In one sense of the word, only the South is really *furnished* to hear and understand such messages.

In addition to the ingredient of failure, a second peculiarity about the Southerner's view of the world is that it builds upon the knowledge, even if he does not readily concede it, of what it means to be *wrong*. The Southerner, in his fateful defense of slavery, was destined to encounter more basic shocks than physical defeat and failure. He was also bound to be convicted, on the bar of the nation's conscience, of moral transgression. Again, the contrast with the nation's normative experience is remarkable, for American life, taken as a whole, has always thrived on the illusion of innocence. If it is true that many Southerners still stubbornly deny the moral implications of their racial positions (see Chapter 4), it is nevertheless also the case that the South has come to find itself more and more fascinated with the subject of guilt, and has had to struggle against the draining claims of guilt even in establishing its argument that it is not guilty. And more than a little nowadays, even the most vigorous defense of segregation is likely to harbor somewhere below the surface the excruciating double feeling of possible guilt, in spite of all that logic can be made to yield to the contrary, and of certain change, in which what is now defended as "right" will be swept away anyway. Nearly all Southerners, save "the most obtuse and insensitive,"

Ralph McGill has declared, "have long carried a private weight of guilt about the inequities of segregation."

Here is a bitingly concrete element of reality: the knowledge that one has lost his way, that his wrongs can be seen in the past, reflected off the deeds of his ancestors; that his wrongs can be imagined into the future, interfering with the goings and comings of posterity; that his wrongs can be glimpsed in the present, mirrored in his less quiescent fellows and focused somehow in himself. The point, let us stop to remember, is not that the Southerner is unique as a sinner; all men of all regions are that. The point is that the Southerner, in a sense, is more blessed than other men, having a concrete experience and history centered upon involuntary servitude and rebellion to remind him, savingly, that he was "conceived in iniquity." Indeed, if there is any one dimension of salvation which the classical Northern man lacks and needs, it is just this penance imposed by history to remind him that he is a sinner, too. Until the Northerner can look back and say about some epochal experience of his: "I was wrong about that," the chances are that he is going to fall somewhat short of the Southerner on the yardstick of authenticity.

There is a conventional rejoinder to all this, namely, that Southerners don't take advantage of this special historical revelation of their condition as men, and repent. They are, touching the past and the Negro, according to this rejoinder, unregenerate, unreconstructed, unrepentant. It is true, we may say, that many Southerners are indeed unaware of this whole issue. Yet changes are now sweeping the South. Enough Southerners are seizing upon reality to make a difference. When a "people" repents, as Dietrich Bonhoeffer, the young German theologian martyred by the Nazis, once argued, it is not a question of "how many" do it, for it has never been the case that a whole people are repentant members of the "people of God." God promised not to destroy Sodom even if only ten righteous people could be found there (Genesis 18:32). "He is able," says Bonhoeffer in *Sanctorum Communio,* "to see the whole people in a few, just as he saw and reconciled in One the whole of humanity."

The Chief Difference

So far we have taken the view that the most decisive differences between the South and other regions may be found to lie in its special history and experience. As if we were penetrating sheaths of concentric circles, we have been looking inward at this history and experience. The outermost ring is the ring of failure. Buried underneath that is the ring of guilt. It is with the next, third ring that we begin to come upon the core, the center of the South's differentness; for with this innermost component of the Southern experience we encounter those elements that led to guilt and failure. Here we come to the Southerner's special gift from God, a gift which he was tempted to use apart from the purposes God had in mind, a gift that, distorted, became a tragic curse. In fact, the theologian might want to give a name to this innermost circle in that vein and call it "the ring of temptation." We can be more comprehensive, however, and talk about the gift and hope itself which became a temptation and led to the Southerner's tragic history. That gift was the South itself, its land and space, its easygoingness and personalness. But that is to get ahead of the logical progression of ideas. Let us continue to reason backward from the South's present state. The special experience of the South that we have been exploring has been compounded, among its special ingredients, of several kinds of misfortune. There was the tragic episode of mastery of the Negro, followed by the burning tragedy of war, the angry tragedy of reconstruction, the smug tragedy of segregation. Whether we like it or not, men build their conceptions of life and reality upon their crises and misfortunes as much as upon their happy days, probably more so. Indeed, that is what the word "experience" means: intensive undergoing of peril or crisis. The white Southerner's present condition, then, is the long-range upshot of a background or history marked in definite ways by his shock-ridden experience, the unbearable triumph of having had his way for a time with the black man, the equally unbearable defeat of not having had his way in perpetuity, the generations-long conflict of mind that followed his defeat, a conflict that only just now shows signs of resolving itself. The point is that in all these ways, in all these ingredients of experience, the South is unique. Its perils have been its own, which is to say its experience has been distinct.

We could say the same for other distinctive groups. The Negro brings to the American society a special history. It is not his racial characteristics that make him different, but rather the special crises he has had to reckon with in becoming what he is today. These crises, specifically, consisted of being subjugated, perhaps being thrown too early upon the ruthlessness of the free world, being rudely disappointed (after Reconstruction) when his chief supporters, the Northern Republicans, dropped all concern for him and turned to exploiting America's industrial resources. Not the least of the collective experiences the Negro has had to deal with must be that form of pride that comes from knowing other men have made you the bone of contention, that they are fighting over you, that they occasionally turn their love of your liberty into lust for other men's blood (or conversely, that they so little show any love of your liberty that they will resist to the death men who try to force it out of them).

As for the Northerner, his experience is special, too: it consists, in the simplest terms, of a millennium earned, rather than a Paradise lost, as with the South, or a manhood to be asserted, as with the Negro. In morals and riches, the North has conferred upon America its normative, standard understandings of what success and achievement are. And the Northerner has his sins, too, no whit less heinous than the Southerner's, but different for all that: his peculiar sin is pride for nation in respect of its industry and righteousness, and it is a pride, as we have observed, that sorely needs the tempering of bitter self-knowledge.

It is not just failure and guilt that make the Southerner different, then. There are more fundamental differences lying, so to speak, at the center of Southern history. These differences are seen in the Southerner's special, distinctive set of crises and misfortunes, his experience. Even yet, though, we have not fully specified the content of this inner core of differentness about the South. The concept of being-shaped by a crisis still does not pin down fully enough what it is that is different. To the special quality of crisis must be added the notion of noncrisis or relief from the crisis, or in short, the Garden of Eden (or Heaven) that would obtain in the region except for its recurring crises. To put it another way, we are now inquiring about what, for the Southerner, constituted his special view of the *kingdom of God,* and we are suggesting that the chief difference between North and South, at least theologically, may be understood by asking what is different about their views of salvation, relief from crisis, entrance into the kingdom of God.

Some years ago, the Yale Christian-ethicist and theologian, H. Richard Niebuhr, wrote a book called *The Kingdom of God in America.* In it he attempts to understand the American people by their strivings to realize a kingdom of God on earth. We must adopt a similar pattern, I think, if we are to understand the long history of regional differences that have separated North and South and have brought, among other unhappy consequences, the long-term, continued racial problem. We must see the divergent Northern and Southern experiences as alternative conceptions of a hoped-for kingdom of God on earth, as alternative programs in regional minds for answering crisis and misfortune with salvation.

When, some may ask, did these regionally different kingdom-conceptions take form? They have been there lying latent, I should say, throughout our history; they have been there as long as the parts of our nation have realized they had special gifts, which inevitably tempted misuse. The more external symptoms of differentness—defeat, guilt—were already present in the South, W. J. Cash points out, in the ante-bellum Old South:

This Old South, in short, was a society beset by the specters of defeat, of shame, of guilt—a society driven to the need to bolster its morale, to nerve its arm against waxing odds, to justify itself in its own eyes and in those of the world.[4]

We can move the clock back, indeed, to any given point —let us say, to August, 1831, a generation before the War —and in germ form find all the ingredients of a special view of the kingdom of God. This was the month when a Virginia slave, Nat Turner, led some seventy of his people in an insurrection. Fifty-seven white people lost their lives in the massacre which followed. In a countermassacre all the insurrectionists died. Here, already, was a kingdom-dream sicklied over with tragedy. The Southerner, who had dreamed of making something of his land, was visited here with the iniquity of his method of doing so. The ensuing debates in the Virginia legislature showed that some Southerners, in truth, knew what human frailty could lead to, once set in the train of self-aggrandizement upon the land; but the majority reckoned the system of chattel slavery to be, after all, the surest way of realizing what God had given to be realized: the South's glorious terrain. The kingdom and the fall of those in it was already in course.

We have arrived, then, at the core, theologically speaking, of Southern differentness. It lies in the peculiar dimensions of the Southern kingdom of God on earth. These dimensions are encompassed in the Southland itself, God's gift of land to the Southerner. Let me be clear. I would reject all strictly environmental or economic "explanations" of Southern differentness. Climate, the cotton gin, the broad expanse of acres to be cultivated by chattel slavery, these were collectively not *causes* of the Southerner's coming tragedy, but rather the *temptations* to it. God's gift of a special way of life was too much. The Southerner determined to make more of it than God required of him to make, and he determined to do so by launching himself upon a regional career of slaveholding. He decided in this wise as a way of claiming himself a world of his own. The land was there for him, so to speak, and when God, possibly speaking through the consciences of the New Englanders and Midwesterners, asked him how he justified his slaves, he himself attempted to use the economic and environmental theories as excuses, plus many others. One of his alibis, indeed, was the Bible itself, for the Southerner at a certain point began insisting that God himself, in his written word, told him that he should keep slaves!

Formally, I believe, the situation was the same with the Southerner and his soil and land and space as it was with the Bible's symbols of humanity, Adam and Eve and their Garden and its trees. No simple "explanation" of the Fall will ever do: it wasn't by her foreordained "nature" that Eve picked and ate the fruit; it wasn't an accident; it wasn't the "cause" of the environment. The serpent represents nothing more than temptation, the accommodating possibilities of nature; he was temptation waiting there for the two human beings, in their anxiety, who fatefully decided through the avenue of the temptation to strike out proudly on their own. Adam and Eve caved in to the temptation to build themselves a world, a self-sufficient world. And when God later asked them why they had done it, they had all sorts of excuses. After all, the serpent had suggested it. After all, it was Eve's idea (Adam said). After all, hadn't it been God's idea in the first place to put Eve in the Garden? Indeed, it looked as if the whole thing might very well be God's fault!

To return to sober history, then, we may say it was not the "nature" of the Southerner to be a slaveholder any more than it was Eve's "nature" to pluck the fruit. It was not the accident or compulsion of environment which caused the Southerner to keep slaves. It was not the ordination of God which gave the Southerner's hand dominion over another human being. The Southerner, rather, entered upon his ordeal of slaveholding because that was the way his good surroundings tempted him and got inside his own anxiety to live and show himself worthy of God's partnership. He could make himself a world of his own this way and with a world of his own he could all the better serve God and even man.

All other men have found temptation there waiting for them, too. But the Southerner found his in his own way. And his unique form of yielding to temptation has been passed along to this very day among his posterity. Not by biology. Not by historical determinism. But by *decision*. For each Southerner, today, has his own choice to make: whether he shall seek life by setting himself apart from the Negro, or whether he shall cast his lot, in the midst of the South's terrain, with the other children of God he finds there. He cannot have it both ways. Inexorably, the choice of his ancestors comes upon him as temptation, too: to follow in their way and perpetuate the kingdom-dream built upon white supremacy. But for each of us in the South, it *is* a matter of choice, not compulsion.

In pursuing this conception of the Southern kingdom and its distortion we have doubtless raised questions. Have we not finally agreed with Ulrich B. Phillips, that the rule of the white man is indeed the "central theme" of Southern history? Have we not delineated a Southern kingdom of God built on just this pretension to race rule? It is true that the motif of "white man's rule" has followed the Southerner through his historic crises. But the notion of white supremacy is the Southerner's *misuse* of his kingdom, not the kingdom itself. The Southerner, endowed with the gift of land and the opportunity for a close-knit, personal kind of society, turned his gifts, through pride and anxiety, into the institution of white supremacy. Lying underneath the false conclusion that a world could be tended by chattel slavery may be discerned, even through the opaqueness of sin, the pristine, Edenlike framework of the intended Southern kingdom of God. Segregation is not part of this framework; it is the distortion of it.

What are the attributes of the real Southern kingdom

of God itself then—the lineaments, so to speak, of the Southerner's gifts from God? I would suggest that they may be found in the following attributes:

• A sense of *place*, which may be contrasted with the Northerner's sense of *time*.

• A high valuation on the *rootedness* and *personalness* of man, which may be contrasted with the Northerner's high valuation on the *equality* of man.

• A passion for *concreteness*, which may be contrasted with the Northerner's thirst for *universality* in the abstract.

• A longing for *stability*, which may be contrasted with the Northerner's hankering for *progress*.

No one will be so foolish as to believe I am now suggesting absolute contrasts between North and South on any of these heads. There never was a set of absolute contrasts, and whatever differences existed in the past have been steadily obliterated by cross-migration, intercommunication, and the trend to new industry in the South. Nevertheless, I think these four comparisons are valid as statements about tendencies in the two regional minds—tendencies which have substance in the realities of history and experience, and in the ways the two regions face crisis.

Place Versus Time

"The Negroes are right," William Faulkner said in an interview. "I will go on saying that the Southerners are wrong and that their position is untenable...."

47

"But," he added in ominous completion of the sentence, "if I have to make the same choice Robert E. Lee made then I'll make it." Faulkner hazarded the guess that his own grandfather had fought in the Confederate army not because he thought slaveholding was right, "but to protect his native land from being invaded." He insisted that he didn't want to have to do what his grandfather had to do, choose between the United States government and Mississippi. But if he did have to make the choice, Faulkner said, "Then I'll choose Mississippi." [5]

What makes Southerners like this? However unsatisfactory in some other respects, the agrarian society with which Southerners first attempted to build their kingdom of God conferred on them some lasting values. One was a love of land and a sense of the importance of place. Perhaps there is an inevitable conflict between this high valuation on place and other human values, and perhaps Faulkner's dilemma illustrates it. And yet, we must insist, the Southerner's sense of place—almost born in him—is what lends substance to his sense of person. It is virtually what furnishes him with the means of becoming a person. It is what made Faulkner, we could say, the writer he was: not his Southernness as such, but his sense of place. William Faulkner, the writer, set out to understand man by starting with men where they live, where they are —not with man in isolation or as an abstraction.

"In other countries," Helen Hill observes, "the capitals are places for the implementing of the ideas of the people who come to them." The ideas, she suggests, come with the man. "The task of the city is to generalize them, to render them effective." But New York, capital of American culture, is not like that. Americans go to New York not "to bring something" but rather "to become something, cheerfully admitting that they are nothing when they go." This "New York" manner of coming to truth omits something vital: the wholeness of selfhood, the assertion of personal value that depends deeply on the person's setting in "a local habitation." But this concept of authentication of personality is almost lacking in American life, to its detriment. American life has "temporal unity," she says, but not "spatial unity, based upon the here rather than the now." [6]

Having a place is central to the concept of personal value. Ethically, the words and deeds of the sit-in demonstrators across the South carried weight because they came from young men and women who lived on the scene, who gave seriousness to their statements by their knowledge of conditions, and by the very risk required *of them* to make such statements. That is why the insistence of one William Faulkner or one James McBride Dabbs or one white college student in New Orleans that "the Southerner must change his ways" has so much more warrant about it than the assertions of twenty Australians or Montanans to the same effect. But more is involved here than the ethical weightiness that is lent by local reference. The very notion of *being a person* cannot be separated from the idea of *having a place*. "The place and its genius," says Helen Hill again, "find their expression through him, just as he must find his authenticity in them, if either is to be found at all." She contrasts the

49

society which has this sense of place and therefore gives its members a confident feeling of what they *are* with the tendency in metropolitan culture to prize a mere "sense of becoming," a sense which keeps a person forever on the way there, but ever "too busy to be."

One sober corollary is necessary: the Southerner's appreciation of place is also a special mark of his finitude. It can be, as well as an asset, a liability; he can be imprisoned by place. It was the ability of men in the industrial sector of our country to free themselves of the rigidities of fixed place that led to our great national concepts of democratic freedom and material gains. Industrial culture has the great boon of forming a society on "free contract" rather than on place or status. But yet at a great price: the economic revolution freed the American from indenture to place only at the cost of giving up roots and of having to adopt mobility as a way of life. Though it brings freedom and a high standard of living, mobility is not a self-evident good, especially today. In fact, at an extreme, the lack of a place can become a destructive attribute of the American economy, even more harmful to a sense of values than place-boundedness. Now that the industrial revolution has completed what we may call its first round, and the fruits of abundance are widely distributed, perhaps it is time to change our conceptions of American participation in wealth and freedom, and begin to think of ways that Americans can share these fruits of democracy while remaining in their places.[7] This is at least an ethical lead for the future. Recent studies show it is the unsettled who see psychiatrists more often.

It is in the fastest growing suburbs, the most rootless sectors, that alcoholism, divorce, delinquency are the most serious. A sense of place, properly sought after, might introduce a healing change of trend.

If the Southern way of life puts a premium on space, the Northern and Eastern mode, in both its industrial and its reformist aspects, has classically put a premium on time. The adequate symbol of the industrial culture's concern with time is the worker's time card and punch clock; the reformer's concern with the same element is symbolized in the "immediatist" as opposed to "gradualist" dimensions his ethical programs tend to take. But the classic symbol of the South's view of time, on the other hand, is no doubt approached in this vignette from Robert Penn Warren's *All the King's Men,* at the point where Jack Burden visits a small Louisiana town:

... If you are sitting on the bench in the middle of the afternoon in late August with the old ones, it does not seem that anything will ever come, not even your own funeral, and the sun beats down and the shadows don't move across the bright dust, which, if you stare at it long enough, seems to be full of glittering specks like quartz. The old ones sit there with their liver-spotted hands crooked on the hickory sticks, ... Time and motion cease to be. ... I looked across the square at the painted clock face on the courthouse tower, which was the clock the old ones kept time by, and waited. [8]

A fully authentic Christian ethics, it will now be obvious, should be dialectically balanced between the attributes of the Northern and Southern kingdoms of God. From the Southern experience comes the God-given insight that ethical statement gains weight and warrant by its embodiment in place. The Southerner's plea to "let those on the scene solve the problem" is not, after all, on the face of it, a mere evasion, though certainly in practice it often is. At bottom it is the same wise, human sense of localness which the Old Testament prophets themselves evinced. It can be used today by the Negro, as when Martin Luther King told an audience in Nashville: "We want our rights here . . . in Tennessee and in Alabama and in Georgia and in Mississippi . . . not in some distant section of this country." On the other hand, the Southerner is traditionally blind to the equally biblical notion of the *fullness of time,* in the same way that the Northerner is often blind to the requirements and niceties of place. The white Southerner would take all century, if left alone, to heal the wounds of bad race relations—and then some. If he has left himself open to attacks from those who favor "reform, radical and universal" and "reformation without tarrying for any" it is, in a real sense, his own fault. Thus when Martin Luther King completed his argument—"We want our rights now" (as well as here), "not in a hundred years," "not handed out in teaspoons"—he was calling on the other side of the dialectic for completion of his ethic.

Transformation of society takes, we may suggest, both elements: a sense of action-in-place and a sense of action-in-time. It takes the radical time-sense of "The Battle Hymn of the Republic," which deals largely in figures of prophetic *change;* but it also takes the place- and home-sense of "Dixie," which deals largely in figures of *loved space.* Alone, each side of the historic American ethic of "men living together" is incomplete and even destructive. Stress on the urgency of change alone will always produce an angry scar of Reconstruction and leave the original victims still frustrated, in the long run, in their quest for justice. Stress on the warrant of place alone will indefinitely defer justice. Both sides have to be boldly grasped together for fully authentic Christian-ethical witness in American society.

Personalness Versus Equality

Our contrast of time and space has established the basic point, no doubt, that there is a "dialectical relation" between attributes of the Northern and Southern kingdoms. We may further illustrate the point, however, by considering some of the other attributes. One is the Southern sense of "personalness" which may be contrasted with the Northern emphasis upon "equality."

"The South remains the region of the country that cultivates personal relations above all others," observes Roger L. Shinn, an Ohio native who lived in Arkansas and Tennessee. Even the great growth of industry and rising "urbanism" have not blotted out this difference, for in the South there is still "respect for the individual personality and a certain easygoing 'personalness' in human relations" (George B. Tindall). And here is Dabbs' way of putting it:

Your Southerner, white or Negro, is put together a little less tautly than most other Americans. . . . The Southerner tends to see people as three-dimensional, interesting in their own right, significant. He is apt to value personal instead of abstract relationships.[9]

This view of personality clearly is related to what we have just examined, the Southerner's estimate of time and space. His deficient sense of time-urgency gives him license for relaxation, a less fast-paced way of moving. But that means, probably, that the Southerner can be more neighborly, since "the first requirement of neighborliness is time." Just as surely, this sense of personalness is wrapped up with the Southerner's attachment to place. The old-fashioned notion of what a person is, Robert Penn Warren has pointed out, is bound to the notion of a local community, of a place which forms a cluster of "shared sentiments." Dabbs has stressed a different aspect: the South can be neighborly because it has so much space, doesn't need to organize people on an impersonal, assembly-line basis. At any rate, the point is that the Southerner always has had and still has more room and time in which to get to know other men.

Whereas the Southerner historically has solved his problem of living with other men by this route of seeing them personally, in their place over a stretch of time, and therefore of seeing them three-dimensionally, the Northerner took an equally commendable, but very different, route. This was the route of insisting, really with remarkable humility, that he was no better than other men, that they were his equal, that they shared together a common promise or form. It is this element of the clamor for manhood that never really occurred to the Southerner, and still too often doesn't. Accuse a segregationist of denying

the Negro's civil rights and he will tell you indignantly
(and sincerely) about all he does for them in the realm
of personal neighborliness. As a South Carolinian told
John Bartlow Martin:

You'll see white and colored little kids playing together
all the time. We live with 'em all day. . . . I don't let 'em
come in and sit down at my table, sit in my living room,
but they can come up to my back porch and talk to me
any time they want to. I carry them to the doctor, carry
them to the hospital, loan 'em money if they need it, do
everything I can for 'em.[10]

The South Carolinian has his point. To him, the Negro
is a living being, not an unseen object of charity or justice, and certainly not an abstract form. He must therefore be treated as concrete and real in the field of charity,
but also measured as concrete and real in the field of
rights and responsibilities. On the other hand, the Northerner has his point too: it is the South Carolinian, the
very one who is so close to the Negro, who is also so blind
about what every human being represents in promise and
before God. So the Negro never emerges as a person, a
filled-out form of man, after all, until he is granted his
co-equal manhood, and this means far more than his
darky's proximity to a benevolent Marse Charles in the
big house.

Once again, we see a dialectic ethic indicated here
which could reunite ideas that have been split asunder in
the divergent Northern and Southern views of the kingdom of God. The New Yorker is willing to treat every
man he brushes on the subway as his "equal"—but he

does not see these men he brushes as three-dimensional men, as neighbors. There is a countervailing ease and attachment to individuals in the South that Northern urban conditions usually would not suggest. On the other hand, it is perhaps the Minnesotan, who has only two Negroes for neighbors in his whole township, and the Chicagoan, with scores, who have something to say that the Black Belt Alabama planter would do well to listen to: and this is the truth that the human beings around us, however few or many, are men endowed with rights both by God and by their standing as citizens of the republic, and beyond these rights, with the correct claim that they are loved by God, as well. There is great irony in the separation of these insights, for each comes from a sector of our country which finally stunts its own view of community by not being able freely to incorporate the complementary view.

A related consideration is the contrast between Northern and Southern preferences on a person's vertical place in society. Students of Southern manners from F. L. Olmsted to W. J. Cash have discredited the more heady myths about the old Southern "aristocracy." But this is not to say there was no impulse toward an aristocratic ideal in the South. In fact, Dabbs claims, the Southerner who insists that he likes the Negro in his place, probably feels more comfortable with the white man in his place, too; "he likes everybody in his place." At one level this liking for people in their places can be but a way of saying that rootedness and security upon one's terrain are desirable attributes of Christian living. But the aristocratic impulse goes considerably further and amounts to the insistence that the community ought to be directed by its "best" elements. Giving a place of responsibility to those at the head of the community seemed but the self-evident basis of all existence and even progress to John C. Calhoun: "To force the front rank back to the rear," he argued, "or attempt to push forward the rear into line with the front, ... would put an end to ... the march of progress." He went on to conclude that the democratic technique of equality had been made into much more than it really was. This point of view has many successors in the modern South:

... The South has never lost sight of the fact that society means structuring and differentiation, and that "society" and "mass" are antithetical terms. It has never fallen for a simple equalitarianism, nor has it embraced the sentimentality that anyone on the bottom *ipso facto* belongs on top.[11]

It is well known that even the North was slow to hand over to the Negro his voting rights. After the Civil War, for example, Wisconsin and Connecticut voters rejected Negro suffrage. In spite of Northern failure to live up to its ideal, the North still evolved, in a mood far different from Calhoun's, along the lines of what we now call "the democratic process." In 1851, pleading for Negro suffrage in Ohio, Norton Townshend put this ideal in noble terms:

If I understand genuine democracy it is neither more nor less than the golden rule of Christianity applied to politics, or to our civil relations—that is doing unto others as we would have others to do unto us, and I see no reason why democracy is not like Christianity, comprehensive enough to embrace the whole family of man.[12]

Both sections thus evolved valid motifs: the aristocratic with its right stress on gifted leadership; the democratic with its right stress on self-government. Both developed serious corruptions. The Southern "aristocracy" was in fact a caste system, with white men on top (many of them none too gifted), Negroes on bottom. Northern democracy, on the other hand, too often has become the chief ingredient, along with a certain kind of public education, of our "mass society" which has levels of social status, but no tolerance for the true gradation of ideas, men, and institutions according to their quality and intrinsic worth. We need both motifs in our republic. I suppose I do not have to document the need for democratic procedure, but perhaps I should argue more about why I think we need a touch of the aristocratic ideal in this democratic process. The Swiss theologian Emil Brunner points out that the Christian idea of fellowship depends not only on the equality of men in God's sight, but also on the actual, empirical *inequality* of men. Men are in fellowship because they need each other. They need not only the gift of love from each other, but the mutual shoring-up and covering of each other's defects. A community of men is a pooling of diverse gifts and talents, a totality of traits. The Southerner's plea for a special place to quality in the midst of democratic equality can then be understood as a contribution to community, and I would speak of its need in just the same way Berdyaev criticized communism:

The egalitarian cult is beating down to a dead level all the peaks of culture. There is no place for an elite, ... Equality is a metaphysically empty idea; ... social justice must be built not on this, but on the recognition of the dignity and worth of every human person.[13]

Southerners, of course, would have to change in order to take this, their own idea, seriously—just as Northerners would. The latter would have to make "equality" less a slogan and pay more attention to concrete personal factors, but the Southerner, on the other hand, would have to give substance, for the very first time, to some of his long-repeated cries for a community built on "quality." The president of Fisk University is quality, and should be welcomed throughout the South wherever leading educators are gathered. The Negro girl from Clarksville, Tennessee, who won gold medals at the Olympic games ought, by her very quality, all questions of race aside, to be ushered proudly into company which prizes sporting quality—and that certainly includes much of Southern society. At the very least she should, for example, be allowed to dine at any restaurant in Clarksville. On the other hand, Southerners would also, by their very standard of quality, have to begin to question the fitness of welcoming reeking and unshaven white bums—anybody, so long as they're white—to the same restaurants. I hope this illustrates my point: that we can improve democracy itself by giving a decided preference to merit and quality.[14]

The Other Attributes

"We are to revise the whole of our social structure," says Emerson, "the state, the school, religion, marriage, trade, science, and explore their foundations in our own nature; we are to see that the world not only fitted the former men, but fits us, and to clear ourselves of every usage which has not its roots in our own mind" (*Man the Reformer*).

"Reform, and that not slight nor partial, but radical and universal is called for," says Frances Wright.

"The method is nothing," says Thoreau, having risen to defend John Brown's raid, "the spirit is all."

These are nineteenth-century Northern minds at work. They sought immediate, sweeping, universal change—widespread transformation of society and perfection of mind. They were motivated by their conception of man and his capacity for being reformed. It was his ideals, his potential for the infinite, his future, which were most real about him. Thus he should be ever changing, and ever being changed. "What is a man born for but to be a reformer," asks Emerson, "a remaker of what man has made; a renouncer of lies; a restorer of truth and good, imitating that great Nature which embosoms us all?"

That is one idea of reform. But there is another. It is seen in this remark of Robert Penn Warren's, made at a reunion of the Fugitives, the Vanderbilt University poets of the 1920's:

The past is always a rebuke to the present; it's bound to be, one way or another; it's your great rebuke. It's a better rebuke than any dream of the future. It's a better rebuke because you can see what some of the costs were, what frail virtues were achieved in the past by frail men. ... And that is a much better rebuke than any dream of a golden age to come, ... The drama of the past that corrects us is the drama of our struggles to be human. ....[15]

Another of the Fugitive poets uses a simple illustration to make the point. A good pastry chef, says John Crowe Ransom, never need feel inferior to an abstract thinker, say, a pure mathematician. Indeed, if the cook tried to imitate the abstractionist, "his mind would run incessantly over the whole universe of possible concoctions," but "he would never concert one of them into an actual dish meant to be set upon the table; he would leave that to a lesser breed of applying-cooks. But he would be a strange chef." [16] One must concentrate upon a concrete conviction, and say about that: "I believe." He must see that conviction against the past. He must assay his chances of living up to it against the hard, concrete world of one's own surroundings and life.

What we have, in other words, is the final contrast between a certain Northern liking for abstractions, and a certain Southern preference for concrete reference. Should this Southern preference be plainly put down as provincialism? That would not be a bad word, John Newton Oldham suggests, properly understood. Where it is genuine, the provincial mind, whether in the South or somewhere else, consists "in the conviction that one's world is centered here and exists now." Specifically, he suggests, the authentic provincial mind has the following merits:

- It emphasizes a few ideas grasped passionately. "Individuals cannot by nature be all things; but they can be a few things with satisfaction."
- It emphasizes the here and now rather than the universal, abstract, and timeless.
- It admits of a willingness to put down roots in contrast with the attitude of the thinker who goes from idea to idea, sticking to none.
- It has an antipathy toward the big, the regimented, the overinclusive.[17]

On this view, the Southerner is willing to see his prospects in modest fashion, in terms of human finitude and even of fixed limits. With this awareness of the concrete goes satisfaction with the limited-in-scope and with the "givenness" of things, things admittedly far from perfect. The strength of this outlook is a sanity and anchorage that stand one well in times of flux. To the Southerner, even the idea of static existence is not entirely harmful, because it provides a basis, an identity with which to enter upon reality. The Southerner, at best, is a citizen of an established world where things are oriented in place, validated by the realities of historical experience, and carried forward on a human, as opposed to a planetary or cosmic, scale. With this view often goes a commendable appreciation of man's capacity for evil, which may be aggravated in his attempts to change the world and become more destructive than ever.

Obviously, there is much to be said *against* this passion for the concrete, the here-and-now, the particular, the present. And the North has already said it many times over, especially in the thought of such men as Emerson and in the deeds of such men as Edison. The opposites of the Southern obsession with concreteness are the Transcendentalist's capacity for soaring abstractions, the Yankee's love of generalizations about morality, and the businessman's obsession with infinite possibility, represented in his assumption of the prospect of unlimited progress. The moral ideal and the commercial invention: these are the twin vehicles of universality and progress.

But again, we have to assert the necessity of both points of view for a rounded Christian ethic. If "men living together" is our crucial problem, then it is men living together in the concrete. We cannot serve mankind in general but only particular men in their situations. We cannot do everything for them at once, but we must work on specific problems and crises. Because we are only men, there is a limit to what we can do at all, and the past is kind when it restrains us on this head. The Southerner instinctively asks a theologian's question when he inquires, dubiously, whether "we can get appreciably closer to the millennium simply by devising ways to prevent economic fluctuations, or by discovering a vaccine or a specific for this or that disease" (Walter Sullivan).

On the other hand, there comes a time in every person's life and in the life of every region when satisfaction with the status quo becomes an ethical liability. If progress is no final solution, it is at least a temporary one. Curing this or that disease, or even developing a new drug to ease the pain is a proper concern of a Christian society, with its interest in the plight of man. It is not enough to be mindful of past gains, but the Christian spirit also includes a call to look ahead, focusing on new goals informed by the highest promise. It is this soaring idealism that the Southern mind does not make enough room for. If this idealism often lapses into a fearful "higher law-ism" that seems to defy the concrete law of communities, and more than occasionally becomes a kind of self-righteousness with the idealist passing as keeper of other men's consciences, that is a risk the Christian community ought to take for the sake of the prodding. A fully Christian ethic embraces both sides: it *amounts* to nothing unless it is a concrete reality; it *becomes* nothing unless it goes on the quest of the universal.

Summary

The Southern kingdom of God, then, is not understood either by equating it with "white supremacy" or by whitewashing this aspect of the South's past. The Southern kingdom is best seen as a set of gifts revolving about the land and personal relations, gifts that were misused to beget the racial ordeal. The implication is not that Southerners are more notable sinners than other Americans, but I will leave the chronicling of the North's epochal sins to someone else.

The South still has its promise of leavening the nation with its sense of the land, personal relations, the past, the concrete. As an ethicist, I would urge that these Southern differences be taken seriously. Unfortunately, I know no happy, easy way the South might offer up its wisdom; it will speak convincingly only as it struggles with itself.

Before we turn to the South's present ordeal—the direct encounter of Negro and white—we need to equip ourselves further with some theological guidelines for ethical thinking. That is our task in the next chapter.

Notes for Chapter 2

1. *The Burden of Southern History* (Baton Rouge: Louisiana State University Press, 1960), p. 15.
2. Ulrich Bonnell Phillips, "The Central Theme of Southern History," *American Historical Review*, XXXIV (October, 1928), p. 31.
3. C. Vann Woodward, *The Burden of Southern History* (*op. cit.*), pp. 17-18.
4. W. J. Cash, *The Mind of the South* (New York: Doubleday & Co., Inc., Anchor Books—copyright 1941, Alfred A. Knopf, Inc.), p. 73.
5. Russell Warren Howe, "A Talk with William Faulkner," *The Reporter*, March 22, 1956, p. 19.
6. *Helen Hill*, "A Local Habitation," *Sewanee Review*, XXXIX (October-December, 1931), 463.
7. *Cf.* David M. Potter, *People of Plenty: Economic Abundance and the American Character* (Chicago: University of Chicago Press—Phoenix Books, 1954), pp. 109-110.

The South and Christian Ethics

8. Robert Penn Warren, *All the King's Men* (New York: Copyright 1953, Harcourt, Brace and World, Inc.—Bantam Books, 1959), pp. 52-53.

9. James McBride Dabbs, in *The Lasting South: Fourteen Southerners Look at Their Home,* L. D. Rubin, Jr. and J. J. Kilpatrick, eds. (Chicago: Henry Regnery Co., 1957), p. 78.

10. John Bartlow Martin, *The Deep South Says "Never,"* pp. 59-60. Copyright 1957, by John Bartlow Martin. Reprinted by permission of Ballantine Books, Inc.

11. R. M. Weaver in *The Lasting South . . . (op. cit.* in Note 9), p. 65.

12. Henry Steele Commager, *The Era of Reform 1830-1860* (Princeton: D. Van Nostrand Co., Inc.—Anvil Books, 1960), p. 69.

13. Donald A. Lowrie, *Rebellious Prophet: A Life of Nicolai Berdyaev* (New York: Harper & Brothers, 1960), p. 417.

14. A disturbing sign of the need for genuine criteria of "quality" in American church life is the intrusion of counterfeit criteria based on class consciousness and social status. Religious affiliation today, observes Peter L. Berger, "functions as an indicator of class. . . . One can at least make an intelligent guess anywhere about the respective social status of a Congregationalist or a member of the Church of the Nazarene." *The Noise of Solemn Assemblies* (New York: Doubleday & Co., Inc., 1961), pp. 75-76. What we need today is a theologian in the spirit of Jonathan Edwards, who could help us to distinguish the true signs of Christian quality from the misleading ones; *cf.* Edwards' treatises, *The Nature of True Virtue* and *Religious Affections.*

15. *Fugitives' Reunion: Conversations at Vanderbilt May 3-5, 1956,* Rob Roy Purdy, ed. (Nashville: Vanderbilt University Press, 1959), p. 210.

16. John Crowe Ransom, *God Without Thunder: An Unorthodox Defense of Orthodoxy* (London: Gerald Howe, 1931), p. 272.

17. John Newton Oldham, "Anatomy of Provincialism: I. The Nature of Provincialism," *Sewanee Review,* XLIV (January-March, 1936), 68-75.

CHAPTER 3

Toward an Ethic for the Situation

... The labor movement once was heralded as the great force that would crush segregation. Although I had seen examples ... of its pushing toward that end by giving Negroes equality of economic opportunity, from what I had seen in Birmingham the optimism was unwarranted.

—CARL ROWAN [1]

But history was forged for Israel in the living situation itself, in a dramatic conflict of will between themselves and God.

—RONALD GREGOR SMITH [2]

Toward an Ethic for the Situation

I AM a faithful reader of the weekly newspaper published in the Mississippi town where I was born. Not long ago, a Baptist minister there placed an advertisement telling the people of the county about two things: first, what he believed in; second, what he didn't believe in.

Among the things he did believe in, he listed the infallibility of Scripture, the divinity of Christ, and the substitutionary, blood atonement. Two of the things he didn't believe in were (1) integration of the races and (2) the "Social Gospel." It was clear he regarded these as twin evils, somehow wedded to each other.

Despite his sentiments, this conservative divine aligns

himself with some of my most "liberal" friends. That is, he and they both tend to see the current race relations ordeal as tied up in some essential way with the presuppositions and strategy of the Social Gospel. What we often don't realize is that the classical Social Gospelers, for all their interest in justice to the working man, didn't always have so much interest in the specific problems of *race relations*, particularly those that concern us today.

Let me illustrate.

"The time is coming," one self-confident author predicted, "when the pressure of population on the means of subsistence will be felt...." At that point, the age will have come of "the final competition of races, for which the Anglo-Saxon is being schooled." *This* race, he maintained, with numbers, might, and wealth behind it, the purest representative of Christianity and freedom, the highest civilization, "will spread itself over the earth." The author even adopts a cynical note: "Whether the extinction of inferior races before the advancing Anglo-Saxon seems to the reader sad or otherwise,... God is training the Anglo-Saxon race for its mission." [3]

The words could have come, seemingly, from the self-appointed spokesman for a master race, or even a Dixiecrat seeking global white supremacy. Yet they are the thoughts of "one of the most dynamic advocates of social Christianity," from the pen of one of the very founders of the Social Gospel. The author was Josiah Strong, and the words come from his widely acclaimed book of 1885 on American social problems, *Our Country.*

Strong was not so much a white supremacist as simply

an American of his times, a patron of "manifest destiny." He regarded Western civilization, especially the English-speaking part of it, and within that the American segment, as the true hope of Christianity and the world. He did not insist on Anglo-Saxon purity in the segregationist sense, but quite amiably conceded the "highly mixed origin" of American Anglo-Saxonism, and thought that his race would conquer the world not by extirpation but by absorption. Still, his views on racial questions strike us today as being off-key and unperceptive. He praised Anglo-Saxons for their "genius for colonizing." He thought other races were only precursors of the superior race. He thought it was God's plan to replace these peoples with "better and finer material," especially Americans. He did not see the yearning for self-determination among non-Western peoples, nor the gifts their cultures could contribute. Divine Providence intended, he said, to make of Anglo-Saxon civilization "the die with which to stamp the peoples of the earth."

But let us be fair. Strong's failure to anticipate our present-day crisis of "men living together" does not invalidate his main contribution to social Christianity. He and his fellow Christian prophets recognized "the money power" as the crucial issue. They set about speaking to it. The Social Gospel left for the future the task of strenuous prophecy in the field of race relations.

This future was slow to unfold. Not even the social ferment brought on by World War I was sufficient to shake the complacent assumptions of most American Christians about the Negro's status. "As a matter of fact," said Robert E. Speer, a noted Christian leader, in 1924, "the principle of segregation rightly interpreted and applied is a sound and just principle and essential to the educational processes through which God is putting each race and all humanity." [4] In the preceding presidential campaign, Warren G. Harding had already set the tone for America. In a speech at Birmingham he recommended the same program that had been advocated by a British writer for colonial Africa: equal rights and opportunities, but separate paths socially and racially, "each pursuing his own inherited traditions, preserving his own race purity and race pride." "Separate but equal" was taken for granted.

It is true that there were always battlers for color-blind democracy and for full fellowship, without restrictions, between white and Negro. By 1910 the Negro was able to launch his own struggle anew through such agencies as the National Association for the Advancement of Colored People. And economic and social forces, from this time on, favored his struggle for manhood. The Social Gospel itself was not always so unhelpful as Josiah Strong on the issue of race relations. Though this issue was far from central in his thought, Walter Rauschenbusch declared in his *A Theology for the Social Gospel* (1917) that faith in a monotheistic God meant an eventual ethical union of men. "The Christian God has been a breaker of barriers from the first." Unlike Strong, Rauschenbusch warned that colonization could also lead to "imperialism" and possible "subjugation."

One of the freshest influences came from J. H. Oldham,

a Christian thinker oriented toward international missions and the new ecumenical movement. He warned, with great realism, in 1924: "New ideas are beginning to ferment in the minds of the people of Africa. The Negro race in the United States is seeking larger opportunities and a fuller recognition of its claims." It was wrong to judge other peoples by Western standards or to deny any of them the possibility of making a unique contribution to humanity. In a day when the "best minds," as he recognized, were advocating segregation, Oldham questioned it: "Segregation may not, indeed cannot, be the ultimate ideal." Segregation means that "one of the two races has an almost complete monopoly of power, and to act justly in such circumstances demands a degree of virtue to which average human nature has hardly attained." [5]

Just as the original Social Gospel had depended on the prophetic utterances of exceptional men, so this emergent realism about race relations was voiced by the few— men like Oldham—instead of the churches at large. Until the 1930's, even the pronouncements of the Federal Council of Churches did not advance, as a rule, beyond the "separate but equal" yardstick of the Supreme Court. A few denominations spoke up against segregation in these years—the Methodists, Congregationalists, and Northern Baptists, among others—but their pronouncements did not mean much, for the depression intervened.

The long-range effects of the New Deal and its upheavals were, of course, favorable to the Negro. But even with the forces of government and history working for him, he remained pinned down to his old place in society for a long time to come. Under Roosevelt's National Recovery Act, Negroes often had to accept a lower wage scale than the one established for white workers. The federal program of crop reduction often meant Negro sharecroppers evicted from farms. Professor Schlesinger has recounted how TVA chose to go along with Southern customs "in order not to risk its central program." It employed Negroes for common labor but did not accept them in its training program.[6] And the complaints from churches were few.

The prophets of social Christianity, in short, were disposed to put first things first, and to be exercised most over such things as "the willingness of barons of industry to use machine guns against striking workers" (Reinhold Niebuhr). The crucial issue was still economic in nature, and the Social Gospel was sticking to its last. When the time had come for the Negro to press his claim for manhood fully (the late 1950's as I see it), he would be able to build on the social reforms worked by the Social Gospel. But for Christianity itself to understand what he was about and to help him with a new wave of social prophecy, it would need to outfit itself with a fresh new social ethic.

That brings us, then, to the purpose of this chapter. It is to point to some possible new ethical lines for us to consider as we tackle the problem of "men living together" in its complex contemporary forms.

Wisdom from the Social Gospel

Before we try to estimate the dimensions of a new social ethic, let us survey, in summary fashion, what is of continuing value in the old one:

• *The Social Gospel massed its attack upon a single, overriding cultural issue.* This was the "industrial question" (Washington Gladden), the problem of "right distribution of property" (Josiah Strong), the unregenerate character of business life (Walter Rauschenbusch). The industrial problem, said C. Bertrand Thompson in 1909, is "almost the only ethical problem which the churches have not already settled to the practical satisfaction of all." Though there was secondary interest in family life, urban conditions, alcoholism, immigration, criminology, race relations, and so on, the Social Gospel's "strongest claim to realism," according to C. Howard Hopkins, "lies in the fact that it continued to regard the relations of labor and capital as the sore spot of modern machine civilization." [7]

Several conclusions are in order. *First*, it may well be that ethical passion comes of single-mindedness, and we may have to concentrate upon our domestic crisis of race relations in the same degree of intensity. To be sure, the socially concerned of our times may feel capable of pursuing several interests at once. But it may be our duty to consider one commanding social issue more basic and urgent than the rest. Indeed, nothing is so false as a twentieth-century reformer who tries to flog up artificial interest in a whole portfolio of causes, commending them all with professional dullness. *Second*, we must be ready to pass from past crises to the commanding one of the age; this means, for some of us, giving up the classical economic concerns of the old Social Gospel, and pressing with imagination and openness into the subject, directly, of men living together. It certainly seems to mean that we should revise our estimate of even more remote issues of the past, such as prohibitionism, and ask if our energies may not better be expended on the livest issue before us. *Third*, in passing from the commanding social issue of one era to that of the next, we should try to avoid too many prejudices about "what will work," allowing, rather, the Word of God as we hear it in the new crises to guide us as we shape techniques of action. Where we can build on the past, of course, we should.

· *The Social Gospel owes part of its stance to "liberal" theology, but was also shaped distinctively by the cultural crisis which called it forth.* To say, as we often do, that the Social Gospel arose out of the liberal theology of the late nineteenth century does not define it sharply enough. We have to be aware of the special cultural evil which commanded its attention—economic underprivilege—and thus imparted to it texture and concrete detail. Theologically, this social crisis was the particular form of sin in the culture that smote consciences hardest at that time; that is why it deserved attention. Thus, we can say that the thought of the Social Gospel was shaped to a large degree by the setting of the industrial movement.

It was an urban prophecy, drawing its orientation out of life in such Northern cities as New York, Philadelphia, Chicago, Detroit, Cleveland. It often made temporary common cause with other reforming economic philosophies, such as socialism, which for that very reason need not be interpreted now as integral components of social Christianity itself.

The conclusions for our current crisis are fairly obvious. *First,* we should not overlook the theoretical orientation which can be furnished us today by the prevailing theological mood, which is, for many of us, some form of "dialectical theology," or "neo-orthodoxy." This is not to say that the older liberal thought will not help us, too. But in any case, *second,* the distinctive lines of any new social ethic will have to be wrought out not by theology alone, but by close attention to the setting.

The Gospel itself gives being and quality to an ethical movement; but the movement is chiseled in its outward details and precise strategical posture by the situation which it proposes to transform. When we seek to make race relations the concern of an ethical movement, then, we shall do well to consider the whole problem in its natural setting. Though there are still many forbidding economic and labor problems, some of them tied in with the racial problem, the main issue today does not lie on economic terrain. Indeed, the capitalist system now seems to be working *for* social Christianity in some respects; it was the capitalist urge to get on with business and restore lagging profits, for example, which led to desegregation of lunch counters in some Southern cities. Furthermore, the industrialization of the South by capitalists is probably one of the notable ways in which the hold of agrarian white supremacists has been loosened all over the South. The time has come, I suggest, when it will be beneficial to address ourselves directly to cultural arrangements and understandings in the South, just as the Social Gospel took its stance upon economic terrain in the industrial North.

• *The Social Gospel pursued its goal by means of a double-edged method; it insisted on external change in society and inward change in men.* Thinkers such as Rauschenbusch were convinced that full-fledged reform of the business community depended upon both mandatory and voluntary change for the better. Enlightened legislation would improve external conditions in society at large; repentance by those involved in economic oppression would add humanity and depth to the outward changes.

It is often assumed, in this age of realistic theology, that the proponents of the Social Gospel were hopelessly optimistic, attaching too little importance to sin and relying too strongly on the voluntary, loving spirit to work reforms. I am not so sure this is a fair judgment. A naïve trust in "voluntarism" is more accurately assigned to the Christian orthodoxy that preceded the Social Gospel. Certainly such hardheaded proponents of the Social Gospel as Walter Rauschenbusch went further. If Rauschenbusch could make the seemingly naïve statement: "We have a divine instinct for righteousness within us that acts as a guide," he could also insist: "I do not hold that the use of force against oppression can always be condemned as wrong." [8]

In addition, the Social Gospel in its mature form insisted on the existence of *group* evil and sin as something not to be dealt with solely by the voluntary repentance of individuals. A Commission of the Federal Council of Churches investigated the South Bethlehem, Pennsylvania, steel strike in 1910. It said the worker was in need not so much of benevolent paternalism and professed interest in his personal morals on the part of capitalists as of objective and fair treatment. In other words, the Commission came out for enforceable standards of justice, as a remedy for social ills, in preference to "voluntary" measures on the part of employers:

Nothing could be more exasperating to the workingman than to assume that he desires to persuade his employers "to deal generously and magnanimously" with him. What he desires and demands is not generosity and magnanimity at the hands of his employer, but simple justice. [9]

At the same time, the Social Gospel did make room for the inward side, the need for reform to strike to the heart. Perhaps it could not always begin there, but must start on the picket line or in the halls of Congress. But it had to end there if it was to count as a Christian gain. No "outward economic readjustment" is ever enough to Rauschenbusch; what our nation needs is "a new mind and heart, a new conception of the way we all ought to live together." On this piece of wisdom out of the Social Gospel, the conclusions are virtually self-evident for our newer problem of race relations, and the broader issue of men living together. We shall need to recall, with a clue from Rauschenbusch, that full repentance in race relations is likely to come only when both forces are applied: on one side, the "mighty and searching" force of "law and constitutions," the coercive pressure of mandatory, outward reform; on the other side, God's "pervasive scrutiny" of the soul, the place where desires and motives are born. We must, in short, consider both *justice* and *love* as Christian modes of action to the end of achieving better race relations.

• *The results of the Social Gospel are ambiguous.* By the middle of the twentieth century, the American working man had finally secured a strong measure of economic justice. But the accompanying goal of the Social Gospel—to reconcile him to Christianity and the Church—was not very successfully realized. Now we must go further and observe that the Social Gospel never even became a generally accepted protest movement in American Protestantism. Most students of the movement are agreed it was empowered chiefly by exceptional individuals and groups, the rare clergyman who was willing to lose his job for speaking out, the town intellectual, the above-par women's circle, the theologian who knew labor unions, and so on.

Not until public opinion, behind this spearhead, gradually began to shift, not until reforms were actually under way, did fair numbers of American Protestant churches begin to tolerate the Social Gospel. C. Howard

Hopkins dates the turning point about 1910, when the Federal Council of Churches investigated the Bethlehem steel strike. But Reinhold Niebuhr, in his early writings, reminds us how churches even in the 1920's remained indifferent to the plight of the working man, or hostile.

There are clear implications for the problems of race relations. We must rely, for the moment, primarily on a comparatively small number of clergymen and laymen to speak out boldly on the subject. Perhaps, indeed, it will be a long time, well past the period when it is a novelty or a danger to broach the subject, before the generality of American churchmen will be willing to deal with the issues of race relations.

However, let us draw further wisdom from the Social Gospel. Paul Carter's study of the movement can help us. Carter distinguishes three wings of activity. There was, first, *conservative social Christianity*. Its proponents were not just standpatters; they knew society needed reform. Yet they tended to believe it could be done by individualistic, voluntary methods—uplift, settlement work, the Salvation Army. (More was involved here, however, as Carter points out, than mere "almsgiving.") At the other extreme was *radical social Christianity*, which thought the conservatives' plan of reform useless. Society as a whole, in its very structures, needed drastic repair; benevolence by and to individuals would in no sense work it. This radical wing was open to the doctrines of socialism and other daring economic programs. Its ideas were influential, but the radical wing as a whole was not able to make itself a vital part of the Christian social movement. Its remedies were too sweeping, seeming to threaten the open freedom of American society itself. Significantly, many members of this wing either left the Church to pursue their social ideas, or abandoned social reform to stay in the Church.

The future belonged to a third group, the center, the representatives of *progressive social Christianity*. Here there was acceptance of the radicals' contention: society *was* in a troubled way and required institutional, mandatory reform as distinguished from mere personal moral change. Yet these social Christians of the center remained very sane; they did not fall for the illusion that sweeping change of itself would automatically usher in a utopia. The centrists, then, neither proposed to ignore the institutions of society, as the conservatives wanted to do, nor to scrap them, as the radicals wanted. Instead, they set out upon the path of transformation or overhaul of existing institutions, always with limited instead of millennial hopes.[10]

Again, implications for the race-relations controversies of our own day are evident. If the conservative masses will not give assent to any kind of thorough reform work, this does not mean the burden rests upon the proponents of more radical programs, such as a kind of military surveillance of the South, as has occasionally been suggested, or a hard-nosed new Reconstruction, or (to mention a Negro extremism) the setting aside of a "black state" in America. Our hopes, rather, must rest upon those groups who live in the South, admit the principle of change, view the present condition of Southern society

with alarm, and co-operate in promoting outward, institutional reform as well as inward, personal reform. Does
this mean we must approve only the moderates? Not in
the usual sense of the word. Reflection will show, I think,
that the "new Negroes," by and large, (especially those
under Christian influences), are by no means "radicals"
in their methods, but have shown, on the contrary, a good
deal of restraint as they go about their efforts to gain
admittedly sweeping reforms of the Southern political
and social structures. I wouldn't rule out the much-
maligned Southern "moderate," however, since (as I shall
demonstrate later in this book) he has been a key figure
in accomplishing some of the most concrete and substan-
tial achievements in the desegregation of public facilities
in large cities of the South.

Yet the moderate is also often indifferent to the inward
meaning of social change, or to the radical implications it
usually has. How many of the moderate citizens of
Nashville, who so admirably supported desegregation of
public schools, were ready to affirm that the Negroes had
the same right to use municipal swimming pools? Often,
too, the moderate is an "under-achiever," taking a line
that his own inner convictions exceed. In that case he is
a drag on the forces of reform, speaking out tentatively
for partial advances at a stage when partial advances are
already accepted and when the need is for someone to
go ahead and speak out for thorough changes that will
relieve the tension. Moreover, we may expect to find
numerous Christian voices in the field of race relations
doing what Carter says men did in the 1920's: speaking

out bravely against sin, taking both sides, passing as "liberal" or "courageous" under false pretenses.[11]

For all these reasons, then, we may expect the outcome of any social reform, whether the Gospel of economic justice or the Gospel of race relations, to be ambiguous. Reform is always a relative concept. What seems admirable betterment at one point seems outmoded and behind the times at a later point. It is not just a question of progress in society, however, which constantly makes past reforms obsolete. It is also a question of the perennial recurrence in the human heart, at any level of progress whatever, of the evils of pride and selfishness. Race prejudice, too, is ever capable of finding a new lodging, always deeper within the self. As one level of prejudice is reformed, a new, more subtle and refined level is born. The transition from the economic problem to the problem of "men living together" is good evidence of this leap of the human plight from simpler to more subtle levels. There will never be, we may be sure, a finished, rounded-off reform of the human heart; still we are called to move in that direction.

Newer Ethical Guidelines

As suggestive as the classical Social Gospel might still be, clearly it is insufficient in itself to guide us through the maze of contemporary problems we face in learning to live together. We need to draw wisdom from at least two other sources. One is the trend of recent theological and ethical thought; the other is the new terrain itself upon which Christian ethics now faces a struggle.

Next, then, let us pass in review some of the implications of today's theological mood for our thinking. Here we shall be able to see at least in anticipated form some dimensions of the needed new social ethic. Then, in the final section of the chapter, we can go on to think about the manner in which the new ethic might take shape upon the terrain of our present problems.

• *Restored emphasis upon the transcendence of God will benefit ethical thought about race relations.* Jaded regulars from our theological seminaries will find nothing striking in the suggestion that we ought to take the "otherness" of God more seriously. This has been a familiar theme of contemporary theology for a generation now. But I do not observe that the implications are as yet very generally applied to the problems of race relations.

The Social Gospelers tended to stress a complementary view, that of the *immanence* of God—his indwelling spirit, his presence in human society. And it was proper to do so. But pride can corrupt what is proper, and pride tempts us to find God most immanent in the highest culture. This opens the door all over again to racial prejudice (Hitler's Third Reich tended to identify German culture and the divine spirit, for example). Worse, it inevitably involves God to an unseemly degree in human foibles, for every human society is beset by shortsightedness and selfishness. The chief problem with an overworked doctrine of God's immanence is that we finally listen to ourselves instead of God. God is free of the sicknesses and frailties of our own human ways, and to speak of his transcendence is but to stress that reassuring fact.

It is not true, of course, that the Social Gospel thinkers left *no* room for a transcendent God. We have already noticed Rauschenbusch's view that corruptions in business life were condemned by God's inescapable justice coursing upon us from beyond. But the Social Gospel as a whole did not stress this view, particularly when it turned to race relations.

Part of the theological confusion among leaders of today's nonviolent movement stems from this old attachment to the ideal of a God working solely by love from within. But talk of the reconciliation that arises from a loving spirit simply does not jibe with the movement's methodology of boycotts, nonco-operation, and civil disobedience. Theological clarity would be gained if the boycotts could be taken as a symbol of God's justice—visited upon an unhealthy society which, far from manifesting God in its life, denies that it ever knew him by fostering racial injustice.

It is God's Word that defines and measures man, not man's culture that defines and measures God. Only as we accept this reality can we hope for new definitions in race relations that will let all men *be* men. God is "the one, original and authentic person through whose creative power and will alone all other persons are and are sustained" (Karl Barth).

To speak of God's transcendence reminds us of one other important truth. It is *God's* love and *God's* righteousness which will actually bring the races together.

Our attempts in themselves will never be adequate. This possibly chilling thought should not freeze us into inactivity, however, or defeatism. We must respond to God's initiative with our best, though it is short of God's righteousness itself. But we should proceed about it with a healthy estimate of human limitations, a willingness to practice forgiveness, and the recognition that before God we are all equally dependent.

• *The brotherhood of man is better expressed through the concept of encounter than through the "continuity" of personality or the "divine spark" in every man.* The doctrine of the benign indwelling of God was so satisfying to liberal theology (and the Social Gospel) that it tended to block creative thought about the selfhood of man. We see why: Christianity, before the Social Gospel, was suffering from an overdose of individualistic moralism. The notion of the continuity of God's spirit within human personality, joining all together, was the way to transcend this individualism. But the result was often the postulation of a nondescript human spirit in which all races shared. Sometimes, as with Josiah Strong, it took the form of Anglo-Saxonizing all mankind. With Walter Rauschenbusch, it took a more impartial, but still dangerous, form: "God is the common basis of all our life. Our human personalities may seem distinct, but their roots run down into the eternal life of God." [12] This view, in a sense, gains unity at the expense of personality—as valuable as Rauschenbusch's "solidary" view of man is, even today, particularly for understanding our group sins.

Where liberal thought did stress the uniqueness of the individual, it often went about it in what now seems perilous fashion, by declaiming the *infinite dimensions* of the human soul, instead of the centeredness of the self. This view led to trouble whenever the personality was, in effect, deified, and hence attention was diverted from the sovereignty of God to an imaginary divinity of man. Such tendencies in the Social Gospel movement, according to Will D. Campbell, "did more to impede progress in race relations by keeping man at the center of thought and action than did even fundamentalism." From our present stance, admittedly fortified by hindsight, this seems a high price to pay—particularly for a man-centeredness that developed the wrong attribute: infinitude instead of selfhood.

Recent theology has begun to rethink the nature of man, first, by accomplishing a definitive separation of God and man. Man is not a spark of divinity or a downward extension of God's essence, nor is God (as more daring minds began to suspect) an upward projection of the best in human personality. Furthermore, men are distinct enough from each other to be responsible and responsive.

But how is man related to God and neighbor if he is a "separate" self? How, indeed, if he and other men are no longer seen as continuous spirits merged into each other horizontally and into the divine spirit vertically? The new theology answered this by the notion of *communication through encounter*. Though God stands over against sinful man, still he invites this man, through Jesus Christ, to have something in common, fellowship, with him. When men become fellows of Jesus Christ, they become reborn sons of God. But rebirth does not drown them in an unpersonal continuity: rather they are intimately related as centered selves are related. Martin Buber expressed the idea by saying that God and man have fellowship as "I and Thou." Similarly, man and man have fellowship not through surrender of selfhood into a vague "togetherness" but standing side by side in common allegiance to Christ.

"The primary condition for communication is the acknowledgment of the other," writes Roger Mehl. It is seeing the other person as just that: an *other*. All communication implies a "duel." Absolute unity between selves, on the other hand, means either that one self owns the other, or that both have given up their individuality. It means one making a "thing" out of the other, or perhaps, as we could say for our own problem of race relations, it means that one of the participants becomes an "Uncle Tom." He becomes, that is, "a virtual absentee."

He lacks the capacity essential for being a party to communication: *presence*. I can speak only to those beings who stand before me in a mutual confrontation, not to a being prostrated, bound hand and feet, at my knees. . . . We have then established a primary condition of all true communication: the respect for the otherness of the other.[13]

In the end, Mehl goes on to point out, true communication, this duel of personality, leads to brotherhood. To attempt brotherhood by repressing the duel leads to failure. The result of this meeting itself, however, is to make for fellowship. For the Christian, "if my encounter with the other is a combat, it is always as well a 'loving combat.'" The meaning of the whole encounter, as well as the meaning of communication is, then, "to make us appear in the course of the struggle as we really are, so that finally we may be able to know each other mutually." Mehl reminds us of the struggle between Jacob and "the unknown" in the Old Testament. Without his night-long wrestling, Jacob would not have encountered God. But at the end, he is "united" with God. Reconciliation and brotherhood, then, come at the end of getting to know each other in our otherness, not at the beginning. Only thus can men encounter each other as free men and brothers.

Mehl's analysis has profound significance for race relations. It suggests the chief difficulty with some of the most popular programs today for ending or curbing racial prejudice. One such view, for example, is that we should imagine all races as being the same color, or colorless, that we should "extract the man from the race," see him as a Christian-as-such, not "submerged and obscured by color and race" (Kyle Haselden). Paul Ramsey questions whether "Christ came to save such apparitions":

The fact is that anyone who saw only such Christians around him on Sunday morning would be seeing specters. He could not see his wife and children, but only some nondescript creatures in their stead, to be denotated Christians as such but with little connotation besides. He would be homeless and communityless, which means that the man of flesh and blood he really is would fade and disappear away, lost in Christ.[14]

Even where theologians now make much of individual differences, they still often seem to slide too easily past differences between groups. John C. Bennett comments, after conceding that "no two men are the same," that "this emphasis upon differences among men has nothing in common with the division of men into races or nations or classes." The important thing, he says, is "the unity of humanity." [15] But to talk about groups, racial or otherwise, as if they were all just alike, or should be, is to argue against the special contribution each can make to society. It is to play into the hands of the theorists of "mass man." It can even be a subtly disguised form of white supremacy, as we have seen, for in practical terms to say you don't want to think of the Negroes as different means you want to think of them as white men. I doubt that being thought of in this way is one of the leading ambitions of the "new Negroes." For all we know, the Negro's unique experience of suffering and oppression may have made him a better man than the white man. "He's calmer, wiser, more stable than the white man," said William Faulkner. "To have put up with this situation so long with so little violence shows a sort of greatness." [16]

The theology of encounter has its own problems, no doubt, but it does have the strength of preserving the uniqueness of the finite self and the special gifts, experience, and history of his group as they engage upon fellowship and enter into brotherhood with other individuals and groups. Indeed, a theology of encounter applied consciously to the South's problems of race relations years ago might have shown people of both groups that the white supremacy to which both agreed did not permit real fellowship in the sense of *men* confronting each other.

• *The Christian criticism of society's racial conflicts can be more clearly expressed through the agency of the Church than through the older vehicle of the "Kingdom of God."* As Walter Rauschenbusch saw it, the Church was not so vital an agency of faith as "the kingdom of God." "The kingdom of God breeds prophets," he said, "the Church breeds priests and theologians." The kingdom of God, as the "fellowship of righteousness" in society at large, thus tended to be an entity somewhat identified with culture, though exerting an upward force on culture to redeem it. The Church, he thought, becomes dry and sterile itself when it belittles the values of secular life.[17] The Church, then, finds itself in serving society.

No doubt he was right, and still is. But there is an opposite truth. If Christianity concentrates solely upon bettering society, it forgets that salvation is something deeper. It forgets that man is responsible to God, not to society. It forgets that the goals of man are something more than having enough to eat, good working hours, better conditions of employment. In fact, the kingdom of God is something more than an improved society. It is the transformation of man from a proud and selfish being

94

into a child of God and a genuine neighbor to other men. It is the Church which has always remembered this deeper side of salvation, and when the Church has been set aside in social Christianity, the program of social Christianity inevitably becomes shallow, strengthless, secular.

As we turn from the economic concerns of the Social Gospel to the concerns of an ethic of "men living together," there is every reason to insist on the distinctive voice of the Church in society. With the Social Gospel, it was feasible enough for Christians to adopt as their strategy the making of common causes with socialism and other philosophies seeking material benefits for the economically oppressed. To some degree even today, the Church has to stand side by side with cultural agencies dealing with the contemporary problems of racial discrimination. But when it comes to defining what it means for men to live together, the Church has to take counsel of the biblical word if it is to be sure of its ground. It is not enough, according to the New Testament, for men simply to treat each other justly. They are also under the seemingly impossible requirement to love each other. The Church, if it makes common cause with, say, the federal judiciary, will certainly be able to make great headway in the drive for justice. But the courts do not insist that men love each other, even after they have been required to deal justly with each other. Hence there is a remaining word which the Church will doubtless have to proclaim on its own whether other voices do so or not, and this is the biblical call for neighborliness, which is a great deal more than mere justice.

It may be objected immediately that the Church, of all agencies in America, has failed to live up to its own truth in the field of race relations, and has lagged behind secular agencies even in calling for justice, the most elementary of the reforms the Gospel calls for. And this is a weighty objection. But it does not carry the field, for the objection is really an insistence that the Church should stand out even more distinctly as the Church it is called to be. It may be, however, that *new forms* will be necessary, in view of the seeming inability of the institutional church and the local parish to mount any broadly successful attack on racial and class barriers; two social ethicists in recent studies, Peter L. Berger (*The Noise of Solemn Assemblies*) and Gibson Winter (*The Suburban Captivity of the Churches*) provide suggestive analyses of this problem.

But we do not, in any case, need to *drop* Rauschenbusch's conception of the kingdom of God as the arena of social prophecy. Surprisingly enough, the Swiss architect of dialectical theology, Karl Barth himself, has given his Church-centered theology an interesting recent turn in the opposite direction. Too often, Barth suggests, when the Church is seen only as being set over against the State, separated from it by a sharp line, the State is left to its own secular devices. At most it may thrive on a vague notion of justice or law. It is better, he suggests, to remind the State that its very meaning and existence is derived directly from Jesus Christ himself. The most

likely way of doing so, he thinks, "is to regard the existence of the State as an allegory, as a correspondence and
an analogue to the Kingdom of God which the Church
preaches and believes in." What can this suggestion mean
for us? We can hazard a guess. The Church does not
depend on society, the teachings of science, or political
theories for its truth about man. That comes from the
Gospel, which tells us that men have fellowship with
each other in Jesus Christ. This is a truth known only,
properly speaking, by the gathering of men who have
heard the Gospel: the Church. But it is a truth, on the
other hand, not just for the Church, but for society, for
the world. "In the decisions of the State," says Barth,
"the Church will always support the side which clarifies
rather than obscures the Lordship of Jesus Christ over
the whole." [18]

It is not as if Barth intends anything resembling the
"kingdom of God on earth" of the Social Gospelers. The
kingdom of God is an event that only God will bring in,
and Barth seems to think of it as an event, really, of
heavenly dimensions. But the implications of his view
ought to be fairly clear for racial brotherhood. The
Christian, believing in the Church's Gospel, takes up the
secular decisions before him and decides for or against
each one on that basis. He has the choice of supporting
orderly school integration, for example, or of not doing
so. To support it will not bring in the Kingdom; and the
Gospel, as we said, reminds him he will have to go
further than the courts in his conception of neighbor-

liness. But to make this one decision at least foreshadows the kingdom of God.

• *The ethical strategist can profit by the recent stress on history, rather than ideals, as the place where God's Word may be heard.* As to the evils of capitalism, Rauschenbusch entertained few illusions; he was a realist. "Idealists alone have never carried through any great social change," he concluded. They fail to see "the solid granite of human selfishness." Truth depends on historical embodiment in "the class which makes that truth its own and fights for it." Furthermore, "at best there is always but an approximation to a perfect social order." [19] Unfortunately these cautionary notes were never generally appreciated in the Social Gospel. It has been the task of the newer theology, especially in the writings of Reinhold Niebuhr, to warn afresh against the errors of idealism. If one criticism can be leveled against liberal theologians, says Ronald Gregor Smith, it is that they lost touch with the Word of God as a historical entity. They raised up the abstract ideal of justice, reasoning that it could be enforced generally; but such ideals were strengthless in changing circumstances and particular situations. They were inadequate "because they were abstractions from the real situation of men." As such, says Smith, liberalism "lost the historical heart of Christianity." [20]

If Smith overstates his case, it is not by much. We can readily illustrate his point by recalling the difficulty the early Social Gospel had in seeing that there was a problem of "justice" in the racial field at all! There was no shortage of ideals; the high ideal of justice was foremost in the hearts of the Social Gospelers. But an ideal is not portable or transferrable; it has to be seen as something embodied in a particular situation or crisis. It is an unflattering, even crushing thought to the idealist, but true, that God not only speaks through our reason or consciences, but that he also picks a more realistic medium to reveal his will, and this is history itself, man's pilgrimage, with its conflicts, heights, depths, gains, losses, and hopes.

"The question of good is posed and is decided in the midst of each definite, yet unconcluded, unique and transient situation of our lives," wrote the young German theologian, Dietrich Bonhoeffer, martyred by the Nazis. It is transacted "in the midst of our living relationships with men, things, institutions, and powers, in other words in the midst of our historical existence. The question of good cannot now be separated from the question of life, the question of history." [21]

The *historical situation itself* thus enters as an element of the decision to be made. There is no abstract ethical conception which can be visualized accurately in its place ahead of time. The situation itself, involving sinful men and their stubbornness as well as their amazing possibilities, is always "drawn into the action and shares in giving form to the deed." The ideal of what *justice* is, for example, is seasoned and cured by the salt of time and place; to discourse about it apart from these factors seemed adolescent and presumptuous to Bonhoeffer. The words may be correct, but they have no weight.

One objection may still remain. We have contrasted ideals and history as the media of God's Word. Does not God's Word, we may ask, come for the Protestant from a third place: the Scriptures? Do not the great commandments of the Gospel come to us above the conditioning influences of time and place? Does not the imperative to treat men equally, for example, come surging unqualified out of the witness of the Jewish prophets, the counsels of the Sermon on the Mount, the calls of Paul and Peter, in their letters to young churches, for brotherly life? In answer, I would say that the Scriptures are not a "third source" of God's Word, but a *first* source, underlying any voice of conscience or promptings of history. Unless the Church continues to look to Scripture as the fundamental witness to the reality of Jesus Christ, there will be no clear call from God at all. But contemporary students of biblical interpretation have laid great stress on the truth that *even the biblical message comes to men in their situations.*

The truth is, God calls us only to love him and love our neighbors; the imperative is always the same, but we see it in terms of responsibilities peculiar to our own place and time. "If we wish to be able to say that we have arrived at the final and absolute meaning of the text," Professor James D. Smart reminds us, "then the outlook for us is not a hopeful one." Such a wish would indicate "that we had no awareness of the depth of the truth that meets us in Scripture." It is true, he allows, that we must submit our thinking "as completely as possible to the text itself." But we cannot know the Word of God except as a "dialogue between the text of Scripture and the interpreter." [22] Let us be thankful it is this way. The Social Gospel found in the preaching of the prophets and the teachings of Jesus mainly a bulk of material critical of America's shortcomings on its use of property and its treatment of laboring men. That is what was doubtless there—for them. Today, our situation is different; the Word of God, we may be sure, will meet us where we are, both to judge us and to teach us mercy.

The conclusion, then, is simple enough: no matter how earnestly or with how great hermeneutic skill we go to the Bible for ethical guidance, the human terrain on which we stand influences what we find there. And that, indeed, is one reason the Bible is a powerful medium of revelation: it points beyond itself in both directions, to God and to us.

Christian Ethics on New Terrain

In *The Operators,* a study of immoralities in American business life, Frank Gibney notes that crimes vary in frequency with local conditions and geography. Denver has always been a convenient headquarters for forgers and "check kiters." Los Angeles is a sort of academy for instruction in the art of real estate fraud. Detroit has always had its acute problems of industrial and labor relations. We might make the same observation about ethical problems. Because the South has been the center of focus for more than a century on the problem of race

relations, it seems suitable terrain for the outworking of
the new social ethic which takes "men living together"
as its goal. James McBride Dabbs is almost exuberant
about the prospect:

The South is a pilot plant, set up under fortunate circumstances, where the white and colored races can learn how
to settle the frontier that now divides them. Here, more
easily than anywhere else, the job can be successfully
done.[23]

Walter Rauschenbusch argued that social institutions
can be criticized most effectively "by men who have
grown up inside of them and know their weak spots."
He was arguing specifically that men who knew the
industrial world and its ills—particularly by past com-
plicity in them—were best situated to lead its reform.
We can assert the same thing for the problem of race
relations. It is the South, with its past of "prejudices,
memories, hates, fears, doubts, misgivings, passions,
hopes, dreams, and gnawings of the heart" (Frank Tannenbaum) which can now lead the nation into the
promise of racial brotherhood. Of course, other sections
may be allowed the claim that they have racial problems,
too. The South wishes to assert no monopoly. Indeed,
racial tensions, fed by increasing Negro migration, are
growing rapidly in Northern cities. In the first half of
1961, for example, Chicago, according to *Time* magazine,
was the scene of more racial incidents than in all of
1960. A Jesuit priest, the Rev. Trafford P. Maher of St.
Louis was widely quoted for his view that mistreatment

of Negroes in Northern cities may be more significant than Southern segregation customs. He pointed to exclusion of Negroes from housing developments, superior jobs, private hospitals, and country clubs, and he said he wondered if Negroes might not find this treatment more degrading than their ordinary experiences in the South.

He may be right. And yet the South, almost by common consent of Northerners, Negroes, and white Southerners, is the universal symbol today of the agony of the racial problem. Though not alone in its offenses, the South in its heart knows it must wrestle with the problem as the deputy of the nation; if progress and understanding can be advanced here, the country and humanity itself will enjoy a symbolic pardon.[24]

But it is by no means the South's record as an offender, alone, that makes it the appropriate terrain for ethical thought and work. Southerners are increasingly determined to solve the problem; the thoughtful people of the region, and I mean both races, are going about it with a new, massive concentration that is unmatched in other sections of the country. I would cite the maturity, humanity, and gracefulness, as well as the courage, of the people of Atlanta, who brought off peaceful school desegregation in 1961 in a fashion previously unmatched. This same metropolis, in five years, integrated libraries, city buses, taxicabs, golf courses, and lunch counters. One reason, of course, was Negro pressure, which also resulted in the admission of Negro students to the University of Georgia. But another was the new determination of the people at large to get on with the problem responsibly.

I have already pointed out that Christian values lodged in Southern thinking, once the phantasm of race is to some degree exorcized, offer a vital contribution to national Christian thinking. It remains to be observed here that these values present obvious points of contact with the newer theological mood I have been describing. Such values were present in the sit-in demonstrations, for example, which illustrated that indispensable grounding of ethical response in time and place and concrete events. The demonstrations were local, part of the community, by and large, and so their witness was given gravity and warrant. Like values are seen in the traditional way of the older South, which has its affinity, too, for the concrete, the historical, the place-bound, the time-laden.

In focusing on the South and race relations as the living terrain of ethical discourse, I am aware that we may seem to confirm the conventional Southerner in his great regional aberration, to agree with him that the race problem is all that counts. This strategy, it may be feared, will allow the Southerner (and others in the nation) to continue with economic subordination of Negroes and the underprivileged, since the searchlight will have been taken off the economic area. I will concede the danger that this may possibly happen. Yet I would persist in my argument. First, it is clear that these other issues, though by no means resolved, yet have receded to some degree and do not appeal to our collective conscience at the moment to the degree that the race-relations issue does.

Again, I suggest, as in effect the Social Gospel itself did, that ethical witness is more effective when single-minded attention is devoted to a glaring evil. I believe the nation now has the capacity to will a bruising struggle against racial injustice and to seek ways of bridging barriers between men. It is not a question of ignoring other problems, but simply of putting first things first.

I would go much further, however. I really doubt that economic conditions, with fewer prophets standing guard, will on the whole work against the Negro from now on. To be sure, there is still shameful exploitation of him economically. But industrialization, in the long run, will shatter white supremacy rather than reinforce it. We have already noted how the impersonal calculations of businessmen have in case after case aided the nonviolent movement. It has often been noted how forceful the commercial interests of Little Rock were in urging an end to racial troubles there—when it became apparent the strife had kept the city from attracting new industry.

Frankly, I believe that those who insist rigidly on the primacy of economic change in the South are pursuing an outmoded economic theory. We have the word of William H. Nicholls, a respected economist, that further economic progress itself in the South now depends upon a resolute questioning of segregation *per se,* as well as some other traditions. "I have become very much aware," he says, "of the extent to which certain peculiar noneconomic factors in the Southern tradition have offered formidable barriers to the material progress of the region and if ignored or unrevised will continue to bar progress."

In other words, direct criticism of segregation now will tend to correct economic underprivilege.[25] The Social Gospeler may have been right in asserting the reverse of this formula, but the time has come when we must be more flexible and see that it works both ways. Proponents of the economics-oriented strategy also tend to think, I would suggest, in terms of an obsolete image of the Negro. It may be true that many farmer-Negroes don't know how to operate tractors, and so are still in need of our concern for their economic welfare. But it is more accurate now to think of the growing buying power, education, and skill of Negroes, especially among the younger generation. To do anything else subtly perpetuates the "Booker T. Washington" theory of race relations. When industry moves in, the Negro, by this theory, is seen as an economic functionary capable of being lifted. He may even be accepted as customer, then taxpayer, then voter. But these acceptances, as Roger L. Shinn, a thoughtful ethicist, has pointed out, are not enough: they do not accept the Negro *as person*.

We have to take whatever risks are involved and forthrightly base our case from here out directly on the Negro's claim to selfhood, rather than on his need, even if it still exists, for special economic handling. Only thus shall we be able to bend our efforts to the genuine issue, the problem of "men living together."

Summary

In Chapter 2, we looked historically and analytically at the South's way. In the present chapter, we have surmised the contours of a new social ethic that can learn from the classical Social Gospel, from the wisdom of recent theology, and from encounter with the very situation it is designed to fathom and test. Because the values of community are all too indefinite until they are "engaged by me or by the beings with whom I am or could be in communion, in an historical situation" (Roger Mehl), we have not been able to work up to a neat list of points that would constitute any fully developed "ethic for the situation." Instead, we must work out our ethic, perhaps each of us for himself, on the "living terrain." In the following chapter we shall examine the toppling edifice of segregation in the South and the Christian's responsibility for hastening its fall.

Notes for Chapter 3

1. *South of Freedom* (New York: Alfred A. Knopf, Inc., 1952), pp. 171-172.
2. *The New Man: Christianity and Man's Coming of Age* (London: SCM Press, 1956), p. 16.
3. Josiah Strong, *Our Country: Its Possible Future and Its Present Crisis* (New York: Baker & Taylor, 1885), pp. 222-225.
4. Robert E. Speer, *Race and Race Relations: A Christian View of Human Contacts* (New York: Fleming H. Revell Co., 1924), p. 293.
5. J. H. Oldham, *Christianity and the Race Problem* (New York: Association Press, 1924), pp. 5, 78-79, 170-172.
6. A. M. Schlesinger, Jr., *The Politics of Upheaval* (Boston: Houghton Mifflin Co., 1960), pp. 431-432.
7. Charles Howard Hopkins, *The Rise of the Social Gospel in American Protestantism 1865-1915* (New Haven: Yale University Press, 1940), pp. 24, 49, 246.

8. Walter Rauschenbusch, *Christianizing the Social Order* (New York: The Macmillan Company, 1912), pp. 326, 408.

9. Quoted in Hopkins, *The Rise of the Social Gospel . . .* (*op. cit.*), p. 314.

10. Paul A. Carter, *The Decline and Revival of the Social Gospel: Social and Political Liberalism in American Protestant Churches, 1920-1940* (Ithaca, N.Y.: Cornell University Press, 1954), pp. 12-13.

11. *Ibid.*, p. 20.

12. Walter Rauschenbusch, *A Theology for the Social Gospel* (Nashville: Abingdon Press—Apex Books, 1961), p. 186. This solidary idea was stronger in the Social Gospel than in theological liberalism, but there is no need to view Rauschenbusch, with some of his critics, as a virtual pantheist.

13. Roger Mehl, *La Rencontre d'Autrui: Remarques sur le Problème de la Communication* (Neuchâtel: Delachaux & Niestlé, 1955), pp. 11-14.

14. Paul Ramsey, *Christian Ethics and the Sit-In* (New York: Association Press, 1961), p. 59.

15. John C. Bennett, "The Christian Conception of Man," in *Liberal Theology: An Appraisal,* David E. Roberts and Henry Pitney Van Dusen, eds. (New York: Charles Scribner's Sons, 1942), p. 194.

16. Russell Warren Howe, "A Talk with William Faulkner," *The Reporter,* March 22, 1956, p. 20.

17. *A Theology for the Social Gospel* (*op. cit.*), pp. 137-138.

18. Karl Barth, "The Christian Community and the Civil Community," in *Community, State and Church* (New York: Doubleday & Co., Inc.—Anchor Books, 1960), pp. 169-170.

19. Walter Rauschenbusch, *Christianity and the Social Crisis* (London: The Macmillan Company, 1914), pp. 400-401, 421.

20. Ronald Gregor Smith, *The New Man: Christianity and Man's Coming of Age* (London: SCM Press, 1956), pp. 78-79.
21. Dietrich Bonhoeffer, *Ethics* (New York: The Macmillan Company, 1955), p. 185.
22. James D. Smart, *The Interpretation of Scripture* (Philadelphia: The Westminster Press, 1961), pp. 57-58.
23. *The Southern Heritage* (New York: Alfred A. Knopf, Inc., 1959), pp. 215-216.
24. I would also subscribe to the pragmatic argument that the worsening situation of Negro life in Northern cities can itself be most effectively treated as a function of the Negro's unresolved place in the South. To maintain that Negroes are moving to the cities and hence that our investigations must be largely shifted there is to miss the main point. The Negroes are leaving the South because life is intolerable there; more will continue to leave in the degree that we leave the deep problems of the South unattended to. Thus the percentage of Negroes in Chicago grew from 8 per cent in 1940 to 23 per cent twenty years later. But the proportion could climb, according to estimates I have seen, to 40 per cent in 1970. Manifestly, the most basic attack on this problem will have to be made in the South.

    It is true, on the other hand, that a partial solution for the South may lie in some kind of outmigration from those former plantation areas where the Negro population is still densely concentrated. In any case, crash programs to ameliorate conditions in Northern slums, however necessary, do not get at the underlying problem.
25. *Southern Tradition and Regional Progress* (Chapel Hill: University of North Carolina Press, 1960), pp. 2, 14-15.

CHAPTER 4

The Delayed Shock of Reality

> The young Negroes . . . are not after "mere tokens" of integration ("to-kenism," they call it); rather theirs is a revolt against the whole system of Jim Crow. . . . Theirs is total commitment to this goal of equality and dignity.
>
> —MARTIN LUTHER KING [1]

> . . . There is no such thing as token integration. . . . You are either for segregation, or you are for integration, without prefix, suffix or affix. . . . "As long as we live, so long shall we be segregationists, and after death, God willing, thus it will still be!"
>
> —ASSOCIATION OF CITIZENS' COUNCILS

The Delayed Shock of Reality

IN SOME limited ways, these two groups of Southerners are alike. Both are small; most Southerners identify with neither. Both at least profess nonviolent methods. Both, unlike the vast majority of Southerners, have correctly assessed the depth of the new upheavals in the South: both know that the whole of public segregation has been called into question. Both, having fathomed this deepest reality, have indulged their favorite unrealities: the new Negroes, that most of us in the South actually *recognize* that "the Jim Crow system is doomed" (Martin Luther King); the hard-core segregationists, that "Southern people," meaning segregationists, "are right both legally and morally" (Senator Eastland).

There the likenesses end. The new Negroes, though open to criticism at many points, are basically right; they are winning; and they know it. The other group, the die-hards, though in need of understanding, are basically wrong; they are losing; and they know it.

In some ways, the group of Southerners furthest from reality are the multitudes in the middle. Many have sensed, at some dim level of consciousness, that the Jim Crow way of life is indeed in mortal peril. But they are so used to Negro acceptance of white supremacy that they hardly know how to think without it, or what faith to put in place of this dogma, now that it is tottering. They get little wisdom on the point from the standard voices of leadership. Their politicians and newspapers, for the most part, are still repeating the slogans of white supremacy. The churches are tempted each Sabbath to face the truth, but preachers are often proof against this variety of temptation. The colleges of the South, or many of them, have shown admirable realism by opening their doors, but some of the finest have succumbed to a failure of nerve at the critical point and have shrunk from doing more than opening the doors of the law school, or the theological seminary, or the graduate school, and so the main part of the college goes on as if we weren't living in a drastically changed world. The result is that the "man in the middle" in the South faces a revolutionary new age with no conception of its profound meaning, and little help in finding it. Most people are either indifferent to the subject; or they accept each change as it comes—school desegregation, for example—hoping that this one will end the confusion; or they drift along in the wake of the die-hards, giving tacit support to racism because no one has offered a viable alternative. Just as there are people who still believe the world is flat, or that tomatoes are poisonous, there are still hosts in the South who accept the segregationist view of the world and live on by this compound of superstition, pride, and historical accident.

Sooner or later, the Christian in the South must choose between the alternatives. How he may do so responsibly and in accordance with his own gifts is one concern of this chapter.

Segregation as a Religion

The Negro's right to attend white schools, protested a Columbia, Tennessee, man in a letter to the Nashville *Banner,* is supported only by the following: "the muck-heads, bubble-heads, block-heads, wart-heads, sob sisters, starry-eyed do-gooders, pink-punks, pin-head punks, egg-heads, bleeding hearts and de-segregation buzzards." I clipped the letter because I found this list hilarious, and also because I occasionally made use of some of the same terms of abuse. Later, however, as my collection of such letters grew, I found something more interesting about them than their epithets. I began to realize that a consistent theological theme ran through many. I quote from the Columbia man's letter again:

"Segregation is not a religious issue and never was. God is the author of segregation. He is a God of segregation." This may seem a contradictory set of assertions. How can segregation be both not-religious, and yet ordained of God? The author's meaning, I think, is this: segregation is religious, all right, but it is not a religious *issue*. An issue is something you can argue about. Segregation, on the other hand, is so God-ordained, and therefore religious, that it is not in question. Here is the way another of the *Banner's* correspondents puts it: "The country was equally religious before the unfortunate decision of the Supreme Court and its rulings have created no new religious law, regardless of the decision of some churchmen."

Here is the same intent: to lay down segregation as a doctrine so theologically self-evident that it is beyond discussion. It must be accepted as a dogma rather than an issue, in the same way that the Virgin Birth or the infallibility of Scripture, for some Christians, are nondiscussible dogmas.

Opponents of segregation have doubtless supported this brand of dogmatics without realizing it. When old-fashioned Social Gospelers, for example, insist in doctrinaire fashion that segregation is primarily a device of economic exploitation, they are agreeing with the white supremacists to the effect that segregation is not first of all a theological issue. The same thing happens when ministers broach the segregation issue to their congregations as purely a problem of civics: "We're not talking about segregation or integration here. Christians disagree on this. But every Christian must uphold law and order." I am the first to insist there is a place for this strategy, for often the minister can do more by encouraging definite, limited action, such as civic-minded school desegregation, than he can by preaching neo-abolitionism. Yet the question is whether he is prepared to go further and say more and put the matter, finally, on the basis of men dealing with men before God.

Too, there is the *science-minded* critic of segregation, who may see the whole problem as a matter which will yield to logic and education. Sometimes the critics will allow the discussion to rise to the level of *ethics*. Thus former Governor Collins of Florida argued (quite boldly, really) that ~~integrated~~ SEGREGATED lunch counters in Jacksonville stores were morally indefensible. Most tempting and dangerous of all to scholars and reformers is the *sexual* interpretation: that the segregationist spirit is at heart a creature of the white man's sexual needs. He assigns purity to the white woman, sexual desire to the Negro woman; he projects his own sexual lust onto the Negro man. This is so fascinating it tempts the interpreter to probe no deeper; and segregationists, in their own way, are quite content to have their spirit explained in this category.

Each of these interpretations of segregation—the economic, the civic, the pedagogical, the ethical, the sexual —has its place in understanding and pursuing the problem. But none of them, and this is the point, really goes to the inner core of meaning that segregation has in the South. Each of these interpretations, in one way or another, engages the segregationist *on his own terms*. The white supremacist is often quite ready to insist that it's all a matter of sex, or economics, or customs. The one area he dreads and resists discussing is the *religious status* of his convictions. Like the letter-writers I quoted were the Presbyterians in Montgomery who wrote their board of education: "We see no reason why this question of race relations should continually be injected into our literature and programs and presented in such a manner as to give only one side of the question and to leave the impression that to believe and think otherwise is un-Christian. . . ." What they really want is to be able to drop the matter. Peters reports the comment of the president of the Virginia organization that everywhere else goes by the name of citizens' councils: "The worst obstacle we face in the fight to preserve segregated schools in the South is the white preacher." [2] To discuss the problem as other than a religious issue is to be blind to the forces which the white supremacists themselves fear most of all.

Segregation is a system of belief that would protect its devotees from all that looms on their horizon as "the powers of death and destruction." It is a way of handling the menace to salvation of one's own impulses and the perils of the world as well. It therefore becomes a holy path, complete with commandments, priests, theologians, and a plan of salvation. That is why professional segregationists, despite their insistence that "segregation is not a religious issue" seem very willing to quote Bible verses at you, mostly from the Old Testament. These are thrown up, invariably, as shields, as outer defenses designed to discourage penetration to the realm of theological discussion. The Bible-quoting segregationist is going after the opposition in the same way as the letter-writers I have quoted: he, too, hopes his verses will convince you that segregation isn't a religious issue. Then you will descend with him away from the holy of holies and argue with him on his own chosen safer ground, of sex, or of popular anthropology, or of Negro criminology.

We must resist being diverted and insist that segregation be discussed for what it is: a religion, a theology. It is, in fact, the unrepentant Southern kingdom of God, offering the same comfortable false piety to the white Southerner today that the institution of slavery did a hundred years ago. It is *temptation*, just as slavery was. It is the invitation for the Southerner to build himself a proud world. A hundred years ago, perhaps this self-made world was an economic world, since the slave was to work the soil and the Southerner was to enjoy his domain, accountable to none. Today, things are different in detail. The Southerner now uses the Negro to build himself not an economic domain, but a bastion of a more rarified kind: the domain of superior status. Except for this subtle difference in the kind of world the white supremacist is building for himself, all else is the same. The theologians of segregation, when they quote the Bible, use same verses their proslavery predecessors did a hundred years ago. The Rev. Dr. G. T. Gillespie, D.D., a theologian to the Mississippi Citizens' Councils, warms over the old pro-slavery interpretation of Genesis 9:18-29, which tells how Noah's three sons migrated to three parts of the earth after the flood. As slavery advocates explained it, Africans were descendants of Ham, whose son Noah cursed in a drunken fit. This curse made it all right for Southerners to take Africans as slaves. The Rev. Dr. Gil-

119

lespie does not find it all right to keep slaves, but he uses the same line of reasoning to make it all right for Southerners to keep Negroes in their place.[3]

It is really not worthwhile arguing about such things. You can illustrate any prejudice you happen to have by shopping around in the Bible for a verse. If the curse on Ham's son Canaan is precedent for segregating Negroes, the friendship between Solomon and Sheba, the African queen (I Kings 10:1-13), would seem to be pretty good precedent for associating with them, and Moses' marriage to an African woman (Numbers 12:1) conclusive authority for marrying them.

If Bible proof-texting will not support slavery, it will not support segregation, for they are two forms of the same rebellion against God and man. Really aware of this, the hard-core segregationists fall back on another way of framing their theology. They know, without having read the theologian Paul Tillich, that religion has to do with salvation from the human predicament, from life-crisis. So they paint segregation quite literally as the way of life, whereas racial brotherhood is a way of death. At this point all kinds of statistics about Negro crimes, pseudo-science about Negro inferiority, fanciful history about the fate of mongrel races, and so forth, begin to appear. But these are ways of portraying the human predicament, and we are still very much in the realm of segregationist theology. The idea is to terrify Southerners about their very lives, or symbolically, about the very life of the white race, so they can be offered the way of salvation: continued segregation. Segregation exists, says

Judge Tom P. Brady, the philosophical spirit behind the
Citizens' Councils, "not merely because we prefer it," but
because "self-preservation, the first law of life requires
that we do so." Hence we can even see the theological
character of the sexual argument—of the "test question,"
as one segregationist I know has titled the familiar query:
"Would you want your daughter to marry a Negro?" I am
well aware of the psychological problems that can result
from racial intermarriage; I probably wouldn't want my
daughter to marry a Negro, and shouldn't think many a
thoughtful Negro would want his daughter to marry a
white, on account of just such problems. But down deeper,
the segregationist has another reason for not wanting his
daughter to marry a Negro. It is a basic theological reason: *pride*. It would tear his world down. It would strip
him of his godlikeness.

Once we see segregation as a theological phenomenon,
we can even discern a sort of systematic theology in the
utterances of the segregationists. Let us briefly review
several of the standard doctrines:

• *God.* The God of segregation is largely a God pieced
together out of the Old Testament, although that is hardly
fair to the Jews. The segregationist has carefully edited
the Old Testament, selecting his doctrine of God from
the worst features of strict Judaism, especially primitive,
tribal Hebraism and Judaism after the exile, when defeat
and outside pressure put the Jews in a situation vaguely
like that of Southerners in Reconstruction. Dr. Gillespie,
for example, cites Ezra's warnings against commerce with

surrounding tribes (Ezra 9-10) to show the importance attached by the "Divine ruler" to "the preservation of the purity of the racial stock." He also cites, and this is very common among segregationist theologians, the more archaic provisions of the Mosaic law, such as the prohibition against mixing seeds, wool and linen, and so on (Leviticus 19:19). The upshot of describing God this way is to omit the drastic reinterpretation of God as Father of all which is supplied by Jesus, and which is foreshadowed, indeed, by the more profound prophets of the Old Testament. The latter portions of Isaiah, for example, roundly condemn the Jews for thinking of God as a narrow tribal God who has favored the Jews only and does not love the rest of mankind.

• *Jesus Christ.* So far as I know, segregationists are well-nigh unanimous in proclaiming their Christian orthodoxy. They are all with the great councils of the Church in asserting the divinity of Christ. But can they really hold to an orthodox Christology? Christian orthodoxy proclaims Jesus Christ as co-present with God in all God's work. As the Gospel of John says, "the Word was with God" at the creation. The segregationist, however, does not say this. He has a dogma, as we have seen: "God is the author of segregation." But he does not go on to say, typically, "Jesus Christ is the co-author of segregation." That is not an easy teaching to get out of the New Testament; indeed, it sounds a little silly. The truth is, the segregationist has formed his notion of God almost entirely without reference to the revelation of God brought in Christ. When he talks about Christ, then, it is about a Christ who has something to say on every subject but segregation. Dr. Gillespie has a section on the teachings of Jesus and the four Gospels; but the only place he relates these teachings to segregation is to insist that the Golden Rule does not forbid it for white men—a negative way of bringing it in, at that. In other words, the tribalism of the Old Testament is normative; the teachings of Christ are irrelevant.

When he turns to Paul, Dr. Gillespie is also selective. Paul approved slavery and inferior status for women. Evidently, we gather, Paul would now favor keeping the Negroes in their place. We might ask, however, why the Citizens' Councils do not advocate slavery and inferior status for women, since it is these views, rather than strict white supremacy, which Paul seems to have uppermost in his mind. In the same way, Dr. Gillespie assures us that Peter's great change of heart—his decision told in Acts to sit down and eat with those of other races—does not mean that Christians should do the same; it is only a way of indicating that the Negro can become a Christian, if he wishes, on a segregated basis, of course. The New Testament, then, changes nothing. But let Dr. Gillespie speak for himself:

Since for two thousand years the practice of segregation was imposed upon the Hebrew people by divine authority and express command, and infractions of the command were punished with extreme severity, there is certainly no ground for the charge that racial segregation is displeasing to God. . . . There would appear to be no reason

123

for concluding that segregation is in conflict with the spirit and the teachings of Christ and the Apostles, and therefore un-Christian.

Christ has little place in defining the nature of God for the segregationist, who favors the tribal God of primitive Hebraism, not even the universal God of the full-blown Old Testament, and much less the loving Father of Trinitarian Christianity.

• *Man*. Orthodox theology begins with the doctrine of God, and reasons from there to the nature of man. God has created us in his image, and we can know what we are by knowing what he has done for us. The theologians of white supremacy once again show how far they are from Christian orthodoxy. The doctrine of the superior white man is really their starting point, and their doctrine of God is nothing more than a God carved out of odds and ends in the Old Testament to fit this preconceived idea of man.

This is easily enough demonstrated. Logically, anyone who read the Old Testament for its statements about racial superiority would come to only one conclusion: the *Jews* are said to be superior to other races. The segregationists, however, draw no such teaching from the Old Testament. They read the Bible, rather, as a handbook on the virtues of Anglo-Saxonism. To them, the Old Testament's tribal stories do not depict the special qualities of the ancient Jewish people so much as the present-day superiority of white Southerners. Segregationism is really a nonbiblical faith which takes a certain view of man *into* the Old Testament, changes what it finds there to support this view, then, finally, fashions a God to go with it.

The one part of the biblical revelation that absolutely refuses to be pressed into a scheme of this kind is, of course, the central part: the revelation of what both God and man really are in the person of Jesus Christ. Just as we hear virtually nothing about Christ when the segregationists describe God, so we hear next to nothing from them about Jesus when they talk about the nature of man. Did Jesus teach brotherhood? Let us lay aside such "shallow sophistries," says the Rev. Dr. Gillespie, as "The Principles of Human Brotherhood," and "be realistic in our approach to this problem." What is this realistic approach? It is that there are two kinds of men. There are white men, who are moral and righteous. "Southern people are right both legally and morally," says Senator Eastland. And there is the Negro, presumably both immoral and unrighteous. "The Negro," says Judge Brady, "is simply non-moral.... We cannot overlook his natural tendency to immorality and violence...."

But the difference between white and black is even deeper. It is an absolute difference. "Of all the races that have been on this earth," says Judge Brady, "the Negro race is the only race that lacked mental ability and the imagination to put its dreams, hopes and thoughts in writing.... We cannot count for nought the natural indolence and indifference of the Negro's nature." This record contrasts with that of the white race, which is, moreover, still interested in its inferiors. "Nowhere else in the world, at any time of which there is record," says Herbert

Ravenel Sass, "has a helpless, backward people of another color been so swiftly uplifted and so greatly benefited by a dominant race."

I have already summed up the theological meaning of this attitude of segregationists in one word: pride. It is not my word alone. Even Dr. Gillespie, the theologian to the Citizens' Councils, has gone quite penetratingly to the real significance of segregationist views: they are expressions, to use his phrase, of "race pride," which he approves as moral and as "one of the mightiest forces making for human happiness and progress." But "pride" is not Dr. Gillespie's word alone, either. It is the word used by the most profound theologian from Paul to Luther to describe the fall of man. "I deem the great offence to be pride," says Augustine, "the head and cause of all offences." Men from Adam on have had the choice of trusting God and loving men or of turning in pride to serve themselves, and they have succumbed to the latter. As if he could foresee what the outcome of pride would be in America some distant day, Augustine also has this to say about pride:

Now the health of the soul is to cling steadfastly to the better part, that is, to the unchangeable God. But when it aspires to lord it even over those who are by nature its equals,—that is, its fellow-men,—this is a reach of arrogance utterly intolerable.[4]

From this fountainhead of evil, Augustine says, all of man's other vices spring, for pride involves departing from God, violating other men, "whilst the soul goes into darkness, and makes an evil use of its free will, with all other sins too in its train." If men want to find a suitable symbol of what is meritorious about their race, says Augustine, it should be humility, not pride; for this was the trait of God himself: "On account of this great sin of pride, God came in humility.... Let man now at length blush to be proud, for whose sake God hath become humble." We need not argue the point, however. We can even agree with Dr. Gillespie: to describe Southern white supremacists, it is necessary, by all means, to say that they have "race pride." All that needs to be added is Augustine's reminder that pride is what separated Adam from God and it is what separates man from man today.

Before I started this section, I had intended to subtitle it "Segregation as a Folk Religion." But I was struck by the hackneyed, repetitious quality of the segregationist axioms and doctrines. All the segregationists say the same thing, use the same words, ask the same "test question," cite the same tired arguments about white superiority, give the same shopworn bible verses proving that the Jews started off as an isolated tribal people. If Anglo-Saxon white supremacy once had the spirit and vitality of a folk religion, it no longer does. Segregation is now a dying spirit; its life is maintained only by a comparatively small number of professional spokesmen—people like Dr. Gillespie, Judge Brady, organizations like the Citizens' Councils. Segregation today is in the same shape that hillbilly music is: it has already lost most of its authentic folk quality, and its modern expressions are the uninspired hack work of professionals. If the majority of people continue to listen to these expressions, it is because they suffer from a lack of courageous and imaginative Christian leadership who will give them something better.

The Rest of the South

"My grandfather had only prayer to help him," a twenty-four-year-old Negro student from Montgomery said. "I have prayer and education."

"We used to tell these kids what we were going to do in the next year," said one of the speakers at the annual Fisk University Institute of Race Relations. "Now they tell us what they're going to do in the next week."

"Today," says Martin Luther King, "the Negro realizes that, while studying, he can also act to change the conditions which cripple his future. In the struggle to desegregate society he is altering it directly for himself as well as for future generations." [5]

Up to now it has been the students—mostly Negro, but with more whites all along—who have supplied much of the zeal and manpower behind the nonviolent movement. More than other groups, young college men and women "have taken our deep groans and passionate yearnings for freedom," says Martin Luther King, "and fashioned them into a creative protest." Such organizations as the Southern Christian Leadership Council have furnished leadership of a mature, church-centered kind for the students. In my own city of Nashville, for example, I think of the Rev. Kelly Miller Smith, a Baptist clergyman.

Meanwhile, as hosts of Southerners continue to resist change, the young Negroes continue to devise ever more aggressive strategies. Thus the Freedom Riders of 1961 favored a more positive and venturesome kind of protest than the sit-in demonstrators of 1960. Such organizations as the Student Non-Violent Co-ordinating Committee (SNCC) and the Congress of Racial Equality (CORE) are groups favoring programs that grow bolder, yet remain firmly within the framework of nonviolence. Generally speaking, however, the Christian orientation of Southerners has forestalled any great trend in the South toward such reckless programs as those of the Black Muslims and the African nationalists. If white Southerners prove hopelessly intractable, no one can say to what lengths the Negro in the South will be driven. As yet, even though some young Negroes appear to regard Martin Luther King as too moderate in his strategy, his warnings that the use of violence would be both wrong and disastrous are taken seriously.

These voices, as we have seen, signal the end of a long era in the South. It had been a long wait on both sides. But now, the South is finally faced with the full reality of the question how men may live together as men. One could hope that the South might take more seriously this reality which is thrust upon it. As a matter of fact, much of the South has not yet realized the scope and profundity of the changes.

There are, of course, increasing scores of young white Southerners like Margaret Leonard, a Georgia girl and student at Sophie Newcomb College in New Orleans. Margaret told police, when they questioned her following a sit-in demonstration:

I said that I, personally, just didn't like segregation, and hoped to be able to help end it. . . . All along, everybody I talked to seemed surprised that I was from Newcomb and . . . pleased to be Southern and on a scholarship at Newcomb, and not some odd-ball Yankee rabble-rouser.[6]

But it is not these views which rule the thoughtways of the South as yet, and they may not for a long time. For the moment, it is the declining theoreticians of segregation who furnish the symbols and rules of thumb by which most of the South—white and black—thinks out the meaning of reality. And that is just the point which should concern anyone seeking to usher in a better Southern kingdom: the chief block now is not the virulence of most Southerners on white supremacy; *it is the lack of appreciation of the scope and power of the revolt of the Negroes.* It is this delay in apprehending reality that permits the old regime still to hold sway, and to defer the inevitable, to squander the South's psychic energy on an anachronism, and to extend the agony of a misplaced concern.

There is the orthodox Southern "liberal." This friend of the colored man thinks in terms of a smooth, evolutionary progress. There is no reason why the Negro shouldn't have his rights, if he is patient, takes them one at a time, waits for the benevolent and enlightened men of the community to apportion them. This type of leader sees red at the phrase "civil disobedience," he lectures his younger colleagues on the dire consequences of "defiance of the community," he urges persuasion rather than coercion, blind to the fact that other great reforms were impossible without both. "Not too fast," he says, "we may lose all that we have gained if we get in a hurry or proceed in a disorderly fashion."

"This view, though understandable," Martin Luther King comments, "is a misreading of the goals of the young Negroes. . . . Theirs is total commitment to this goal of equality and dignity. And for this achievement they are prepared to pay the costs—whatever they are."

There is the less liberal Southerner who thinks the Negro ought to be satisfied if he wins a single victory. If he has been admitted to the public library, it is ingratitude for him now to demand to swim with the whites. This viewpoint, of course, even more seriously misunderstands what is going on. The "new Negro" is not a patron of symbolic victory; he is out to restructure reality in Southern public places, and he is going to do it with or without the help of self-styled Southern liberals. The new Negroes rightly do not figure they have to ask self-appointed gatekeepers for rights the Constitution says they already have. But a surprising number of Southerners have not seen this relatively simple point, even so late.

There is the unrealistic Negro himself, such as the middle-class businessman in Atlanta or Birmingham. He finds that segregation pays, and so he willingly assents to the white man's fictions. The Montgomery bus boycott demonstrated how important a role the adult working Negro and even the middle-class Negro could play in pressing for a new way of life. Yet all too many members of the Negro working and middle classes not only remain indifferent, but actually discourage any "rocking the boat," content with their well-to-do, though segregated, status. Perhaps more than any other single group, it is the prospering Negro who gives the most false encouragement to the architects of white supremacy, by his support of the illusion that some "solution" can be achieved short of a much-changed Southland. The signs are multiplying that the revolt of the "new Negroes" has been largely unsuccessful right here with the "black bourgeoisie," that a lack of communication exists with these Southerners as with others. In the end they, too, must choose between the alternatives, and either affirm the Negro's manhood or deny it.

Then there are the more unmoved varieties of white Southerners. Most numerous of all are the small-towners in the South who concede with a shrug that school integration may be put over on helpless city folks, but never on them. Great numbers of them, I know from personal experience, are entirely sincere when they say they don't think "living together" under integration will work. I agree with Arthur Schlesinger, Jr., who comments in the Foreword to Martin's *The Deep South Says "Never"*:

Nor is the problem to be solved by supposing that the leaders of the Southern resistance are evil men, animated by mean and contemptible motives. This was the old abolitionist fallacy. Life is more complicated.... They are (most of them) ... decent men trapped in a tragedy of history.[7]

Sometimes I do wonder if these segregationists are not resorting to deliberate equivocation. They tend to reason, for example, whenever the question of Negro citizenship, say his voting rights, comes up: what the Negro is really asking for is not the right to vote but the right to come home with you. Hence the conclusion: "The real trouble makers are the ones who push in where they are not wanted, the ones who want to make others associate with them against their wishes." This seems slack logic to me. But I know it makes sense, somehow, to many Southerners. And I am convinced that nothing but the force of history, bearing down the changes upon the small towns of the South, will change some. But even in that case, such Southerners are in for an awakening sooner or later—sooner, judging by the pace of events.

Most unrealistic of all, in some ways, are Southern church people. Baptist deacons in Dothan, Alabama, a sizeable farming city near my part of West Florida, became fevered when Martin Luther King made a speech on the campus of their denomination's seminary in Louisville. Though it will seem hysteria even to them in a few years, they harangued the church into voting, 219 to 57, to withdraw financial support from the seminary. One elderly leader in this cause, a banker, wrote the president of the seminary, bitterly protesting King's appearance on the campus. His letter is almost a monument to the lack of awareness among small-town Southern Christians of the crucial issues that are being decided all around them: to him, King is no more than "a smart publicity seeker" and an "agitator." Until King and his kind came, "both races in the South were living under the finest racial adjustment this world has ever known." The seminary would do well "to confine its activities to the purposes for which it was founded, among which are to equip prospective ministers to go out into the world, teach the Bible, strive to convert the unsaved and spread the Gospel. . . ."

And yet, I know, this old gentleman is sincere. He is not trying to evade the issue when he interprets the Good Samaritan story as meaning only that white men should do little favors for Negroes. Christ "praised the Good Samaritan and would praise us for helping a colored brother in trouble." To my friend, the parable actually has no more significance than that.

The appropriate reaction to such old Christian gentlemen as this is not to preach at them for their sinfulness. It is, rather, to note gratefully that the coming generation of Southerners has a wider corner on reality. It is to try to understand the younger ones who still, or as yet, have not been able to break through the bonds of a century.[8]

More tragic than any other group we have glanced at are the countless victims of segregation—the illiterate, inert, poverty-stricken Negroes of the shack in the countryside and the "quarters" in the small town and the tenement in the cities. Kept so low that hope rarely takes the form of aspiration, these Negroes seek release in sensuality and cheap pleasures—and thereby furnish the normative image for the whole of Negrodom in the minds of many white Southerners. John Howard Griffin's *Black Like Me* contains some poignant descriptions of such people. His skin treated so he would pass as a Negro, Griffin visited Hattiesburg, Mississippi, and stopped at a dirty, gaudy Negro café. To white men of the South, the existence of such places is taken as evidence that the Negro is content with his life as it is. Having become, in a sense, part of such a place, Griffin realized that the abandoned music and night life here told the story not of the Negro's happiness but rather of "the immense melancholy that hung over the quarter, so oppressive that men had to dull their sensibilities in noise or wine or sex or gluttony in order to escape it." [9]

This unsavory sector of Southern life is not only ordained by the segregationist system; it is also kept in being by a distressingly large number of unscrupulous Negro clergymen, fast-talking insurance salesmen, and the wealthy Negroes we have already mentioned. Doubtless many of the Negroes would still lead shiftless and unwholesome lives if segregation in all its forms were removed forthwith. That is a safe prediction because so many white people, unsegregated, nonetheless lead shiftless and unwholesome lives. Yet the way of segregation distorts existence needlessly for millions, not only in the South but in Northern slums as well.

The Notorious Moderate

I have saved one type of Southerner for more detailed attention. This is the citizen who is enthusiastic neither about insolent resistance nor about pronounced social change. Only a few of his number might actually be content to call themselves "moderates," and the type varies tremendously. Still, I believe we can discuss him as a type.

Let us begin on the right wing, with the Southerner who is actually a conservative, strictly speaking, rather than a moderate, but who belongs in this discussion just the same. I have in mind the respectable Southerner who is reacting to change merely with resignation. His reaction is, in a sense, apathetic, at least by comparison with those Southerners of marginal soundness of mind (there aren't many around now) who still fancy they can stop change by whipping Negroes and burning school buildings. It is a defensive reaction, for it is often attended by great and righteous protest of the iniquities of agitators and outsiders. It is, finally, at least among careful thinkers of the type I have in mind, a tragic reaction, for many Southerners are apparently going to "uphold law and order," and thus yield at every point to the Negro, failing in the end to be redeemed personally or internally by such public-spiritedness, but only falling back into a kind of regional brooding. James Jackson Kilpatrick puts this mood well:

A sharpened sense of the Negro's rights and grievances is accompanied by a double-sharpened sense of what are seen by white Southerners as their rights and grievances. ... The bus lines have abandoned Jim Crow, but fewer persons ride the buses. Lunch counters are integrated, but there are more private clubs.[10]

Things do change, Kilpatrick goes on, they are really different nowadays. But what is the consequence, under the circumstances? "I sometimes wonder if my children will not know in the South a society far more deeply separated than the society in which I was reared, in which the races are neither friends nor enemies, but only strangers." Though we are among conservative minds with this mood, yet we are in a different world from Judge Brady and the Rev. Dr. Gillespie, the theologians to the Citizens' Councils. Men like Kilpatrick come much closer to depicting the respectable Southern mind today than either the rabid segregationists, on the one hand, or the cheerful optimists among the desegregationists, on the other. Despite his Stoic approach, he does recognize the principle of change and he knows the realities well. We can only wonder: to what extent is his realism shared in the South by other respectable citizens?

There are some clues. *The Deep South Says "Never"* is the name of a book that appeared a few years ago. It was written by a competent reporter, John Bartlow Martin. It is already apparent that the book was misnamed, that Southern resistance to school desegregation was not as formidable as it then seemed to be. Martin wrote in 1957 that desegregation could probably not be accomplished in the Deep South "in the foreseeable future." In Alabama, Georgia, South Carolina, and Mississippi, he thought, desegregation "is wholly impossible." But by 1961 one of these "impossible" states, Georgia, had accepted Negro undergraduates in its state university at Athens and in its famous engineering school, Georgia Tech, voluntarily in the latter. Atlanta public schools had begun desegregation in one of the quietest such transitions in the entire post-1954 South.

It may be that in 1957 the Citizens' Councils were "the most powerful single private force for maintaining segregation." But I doubt that it has ever been true that most Southerners approve of the Councils, as Martin contends, and it is certainly not so today. The Councils have had a difficult time, even with the help of politicians and Dixiecrat newspapers, in propping up the old segregationist world-view. The Councils have been heard by default of other voices.

The Gallup Poll, never an infallible sounder of the public mind, has nevertheless turned up revealing data about Southerners. In August, 1957, the poll found that forty-five per cent of Southerners regarded general desegregation as inevitable. A year later, the percentage had grown, now to fifty-three per cent. After Louisiana and Georgia began desegregating their public schools, another round of the poll in January, 1961, indicated that no less than seventy-six per cent of Southerners thought desegregation of public facilities was on the way; only nineteen per cent now regarded it as unlikely.[11] Even if the poll is accurate, this does not mean Southerners have become either realists or desegregationists: many who abstractly regard segregation as of limited life-span dislike the thought of its passing and tend to repress the problem, refusing to apply any forehanded consideration of it to their own communities. Nevertheless, this shift in openness toward the future is significant.

"The majority of the community are neither extreme segregationists nor extreme desegregationists." This is the conclusion reached by a team of social scientists from Princeton University who studied attitudes toward desegregation expressed by 287 white males in Guilford County, North Carolina. According to the evidence, some fifteen to twenty per cent of the people were ranged at either end of the scale of attitude; sixty to seventy per cent were in the middle range of readiness. This readiness, by the way, was found to be present despite a widespread unfavorable image of the Negro.[12] We might guess that this feeling supports our previous conclusion: the bad images in people's mind about race relations are kept there somewhat artificially by the hack work of professional segregationists; determined leadership could render the images ineffective. Those most ready for desegregation were workers with college education, who earned $6,000 a year or more, who were exposed to three or more mass media, and who tended toward professional and white-collar occupations. Christian leaders ought to recognize these statistics, for they sound ominously like a description of the same great middle-class group which forms a great part of the strength of Protestantism. Thus the question is raised whether Christian leadership in the church—courageously asserted now—might not bring about surprising changes on the subject of "men living together" in the South. If no commanding voice comes, despite the readiness for change which this study suggests, these people will continue to cling, for want of a better cause, to the discredited and expiring dogmas of segregation.

We have now raised, however, one of the thorniest questions of all: does the so-called "moderate" really have any role to play in the desegregation struggle? The testimony against him is heavy and critical. Carl Rowan scores the "haloed liberals" and other white Southerners, supposedly men of good will, who actually "impede progress" by their cries: "We can't solve this problem overnight," "Let us alone, this is our problem," "This would do more harm than good," and so on. It doesn't take much courage, he points out, to deplore violence, to criticize the worst bigots. But then, many white Southerners, once they have taken this step, rest there—"on their laurels." Only a few go further, and these are not the moderates, nor even the "liberals," because what is required, says Rowan, is to say "that segregation is the root and perpetrator of all the evils previously denounced." In the same vein, Dan Wakefield comments that the term "moderate" is usually most popular in cities that "have yet to face a showdown on integration." In the absence of an actual crisis, it is a luxury people can afford, but yet "not exactly a flaming slogan calculated to inspire or offend." [13]

The word "moderate," itself, perhaps, is an emotional term which should be dropped. Nevertheless, there is a place for the moderate, if we mean by this someone who favors flexibility of means rather than withdrawal of principle. One can be absolutely in favor of justice and yet properly seek finite, civilized means, located in time and space, of carrying out one's reforms. The Social Gospel movement depended upon both "radical" and "middle of the road" wings to carry out its total program, the former to jar society and convince it of the need for reform, the latter to find concrete ways of going about actual reforming. The same is evidently true of the abolitionist crusade of the nineteenth century. Louis Filler, author of a penetrating study of it, reminds us: "the abolitionists themselves were often less than the unyielding

140

absolutists their principles suggested." This does not mean
they favored freeing only half the slaves, or only half-
freeing all the slaves. It does mean they saw the necessity
of struggling within the real situations of society and
politics if they were to make more than noble abstractions out of their ideals. Success really meant acceptance
of the widest spectrum of assistance: "Moderates and
extremists, it is difficult to see that the abolitionist campaign—summing up as it did the basic principles of reform—could have triumphed without all of them." [14]

A like coalition, I take it, is important today. If some
"extremists" in the field of race relations are not aware
of their need of the "moderate," or even the silent fol-
lower, the extreme segregationists are indeed aware of
the dangers—to them—of the same elements. As one right-
winger complained to the Nashville *Banner:* "Gradual integration is merely a sneaky way of accomplishing the
fatal result, which is demonstrably the annihilation of
civilization and culture." Whereupon the writer rakes
over all moderates, for favoring "slow" poison instead of
"swift" poison.

The struggle for justice, Richard H. Rice suggests,
should be based on two kinds of prophecy, the prophecy
of words and the prophecy of actions. The prophet of
words is someone who can and will say that the evil of
segregation is the center of the trouble. The spokesman
who speaks out, however boldly, for (at most) law and
order really is not rendering full prophecy for this cause
in his words. But on the other hand, the prophet of action
makes his witness by the action itself, and if the actions

of moderates happen to be actions which witness for justice, *as between alternatives in the given situation,* they are just as truly "prophecy" as the most impassioned reform talk.

Thus, when leading citizens of Atlanta spoke about "law and order" as a basis for desegregating schools, they had made a good start, but they were not necessarily delivering very convincing testimony on behalf of color-blind democracy itself. Yet when these same citizens manfully saw to it that school desegregation was started smoothly, their actions, though the actions of moderates, were still actions of prophecy in the cause of justice. The Louisville *Courier-Journal,* in an eloquent editorial, called for desegregated lunch counters. Its reason? Not because it would advance the Christian kerygma so much, or the cause of integration, but because it would enhance Louisville's reputation as a reasonable, progressive city. This is, manifestly, a counsel of moderation. Should the paper's contribution to desegregation therefore be questioned? Not in my book.

It takes both forces, then—verbal prophecy and the less spectacular prophecy of finite action—to make the witness full. To be sure, if both attributes can be combined in the same leader or group, so much the better. But in actual situations, the labor very often has to be divided. I would not, therefore, reject the contribution of the notorious "moderate" *ipso facto.*

Another caution is in order. Often a person who starts out as the mildest moderate ends as a most courageous witness to his cause. Moncure Daniel Conway, a Southerner who became a vigorous critic of slavery, spoke of such transitions in the human spirit: "One who starts out at twenty to think for himself and pursue truth is likely to discover at seventy that one third of his life was given to error, another to exchanging it for other error, and the last third to efforts to unsay and undo the mistakes of the other two thirds." [15] In our day of faster-spaced social change, the revision of one's views need not take so long. The advent of sit-in demonstrations, for example, became a source of swift "updating into reality" for many Southerners who had thought until then that the barely perceptible forward motion of gradualism was going to solve all the South's racial problems. The point is a simple one: let us not disavow the mild-mannered man of good will if his moderation is accompanied by tangible, concrete actions, no matter how little of the kingdom of God he seems to be willing to shoulder at the moment. He may change; even if he does not, he may be doing the very thing in a given circumstance that serves justice best. And indeed, let us remember, the verbal prophecy of the radical reformer may be cheap indeed—if he is miles from the nearest Southern courthouse town.

Finally, let us remember the relative character of all labels applied to man as a political and social animal. Men from every point on the continuum are capable of making decisions in specific circumstances in favor of justice. We should not in effect discourage them or our own hopes by submerging them under labels. Perhaps a better word to identify the prophet than any of these right-center-left labels such as "conservative," "moderate," "liberal," is the simple word "responsible."

Exactly what the responsibilities of individual men are in the coming years, no one can lay down in advance. The general directions of what it will take to be responsible are clear enough. The South is emerging from a long and fantastic repression of reality. The "new Negro" as well as the courts of the land have thrust reality upon us at last. The responsible attitude, we can say, at least is now to concede that Jim Crow is not going to be able to serve as the *modus operandi* in the South for long. Christian leaders, both lay and clerical, are under special obligation to be realistic on this point.

Summary

In this chapter, we have looked theologically at segregation, the unrepentant Southern kingdom of God. We found it to be a regional variety of the inevitable fall of man that has occurred in all regions and lands, expressive in the South's own special way of proud independence of God and revolt against men. Fortunately, there is another Southern kingdom, one which regards the land, the South's space, its love of home and place, its sense of personalness and the concrete, as warm and human gifts to be used in the service of God and man. Today this real kingdom of God is being accepted by the Southerner. The signs of its coming are identical, under the circumstances, with the Southerner's hand of fellowship put out to the Negro. The required transformation will not make the Southerner into a warmed-over Yankee, nor deprive him of those special, concrete, personal ways of life that mark Southern society. Instead it will let the Southerner use his style of life to be *with* other men instead of apart from them.

Our most important task remains for the final chapter. It is not enough to call for the choice between segregation and desegregation of Southern society. The Christian can never stop at that point. He must ask himself what he can do personally about the challenge that lies at the heart of life—the challenge of men living together. How may white and Negro live together in the South as genuine neighbors? To that question we now turn.

Notes for Chapter 4

1. "The Time for Freedom Has Come," *The New York Times Magazine*, September 10, 1961, pp. 25, 119.
2. William Peters, *The Southern Temper* (New York: Doubleday & Co., Inc., 1959), p. 102.
3. Quotations in this chapter from segregationist thinkers, especially in the remainder of this section, are based in part on the following publications of the Association of Citizens' Councils of Mississippi, Greenwood, Miss.: James O. Eastland, "We've Reached Era of Judicial Tyranny"; Judge Tom P. Brady, "Segregation and the South"; G. T. Gillespie, "A Christian View on Segregation"; Herbert Ravenal Sass, "Mixed Schools and Mixed Blood."
4. Augustine, *On Christian Doctrine*, I, 23; Commentaries on Psalms, XIX:15, second exposition.
5. *Christian Science Monitor*, July 5, 1961; Martin Luther King, "The Time for Freedom Has Come," *The New York Times Magazine*, September 10, 1961, p. 118.
6. *Look*, January 3, 1961, offprint.

7. By John Bartlow Martin (New York: Houghton Mifflin Co.—Ballantine Books, 1957).

8. The more unyielding the segregationist's sentiments, the more massively out of touch he is likely to be with other areas of reality. Thus a Mississippi Congressman, not surprisingly, was one of the few people in this country who suggested in 1961 that Russian space flights, in which men were orbited around the earth, might be "hoaxes."

   I have not considered one other type of Southern unrealist: the rightist intellectual, Southerners cut to the pattern of the old Vanderbilt Agrarians. I would stand with these conservatives on one of their main contentions, to wit, that there was and is a notion of quality in the South that is to be defended. But these thinkers do not realize, I believe, that segregation is the worst of all possible ways to conserve this aspect of the Southern heritage. It is not the community leaders of good background, for example, who are the most effective defenders of white supremacy now; that task falls to the bourgeois and occasionally, in the streets, to lower-class mob elements—the rough class of women who opposed school desegregation in New Orleans, the blond hoodlums who harassed sit-demonstrators, and so forth. Surely the neo-Agrarians of the South have realized that to defend the racial integrity of moving picture theaters and hamburger stands has little to do with preserving the quality features of Southern culture. Moreover, it is not the Negro, in my opinion, who constitutes the chief threat to the quality of the Southern past; that threat is more adequately represented in the ambitions of the middle class, regardless of color.

9. John Howard Griffin, *Black Like Me* (Boston: Houghton Mifflin Co., 1961), p. 73.

10. James Jackson Kilpatrick, "The South Sees Through New Glasses," *The National Review* (150 East 35th Street,

New York 16, N.Y.), X, March 11, 1961, p. 141. Kilpatrick's theory that change estranges the races will be more closely examined in the next chapter.

11. Nashville *Tennessean*, February 12, 1961.
12. Melvin L. Tumin, *Desegregation: Resistance and Readiness* (Princeton: Princeton University Press, 1958), pp. 180, 190.
13. Carl T. Rowan, *South of Freedom* (New York: Alfred A. Knopf, Inc., 1952), pp. 204-205; Dan Wakefield, *Revolt in the South* (New York: Grove Press, Inc.—Evergreen Target Books, 1960), p. 67.
14. Louis Filler, *The Crusade Against Slavery 1830-1860* (New York: Harper & Brothers, 1960), p. 279.
15. Quoted in Jay B. Hubbell, *The South in American Literature* (Durham: Duke University Press, 1954), p. 409.

CHAPTER 5

Beyond Desegregation

> Segregation is dead. It's gone, but
> they won't believe it down here.
> ... What worries me is that there
> is no exploration of what we're go-
> ing to do.... What we must do
> now is find a way to replace a way
> of life that is gone.
>
> —SOUTH CAROLINIAN quoted in
> *The Deep South Says "Never"* [1]

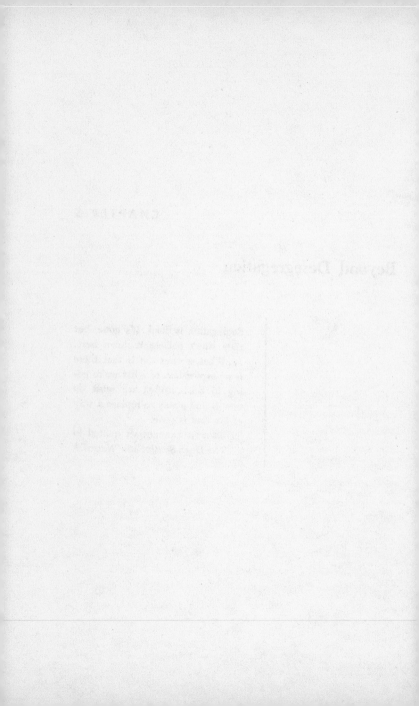

Beyond Desegregation

ON A fishing trip I ran into a vacationing steel-company employee from Birmingham. He asked me how things were going in Nashville. Actually, they weren't going so well. We had gotten used to seeing silent young Negroes at the entrances to lunch counters, legions of policemen the city had strewn along "Dime Store Row" on Fifth Avenue, tragic bands of sideburned white hoodlums who hung on sullenly. True, the demonstrations had just ceased, and numerous lunch counters were henceforth to be open to Negroes. But nerves had been rubbed raw and feelings rumpled. I had come away from Nashville during a dreadful crisis at my own place of employ-

151

ment, Vanderbilt University, for acrid controversy had exploded when a Negro student who had been an adviser to the demonstrators was removed from classes. (He was shortly invited to return and finish his degree course, I am glad to say.)

My fisherman friend heard me out. Then, gently, not at all like the stereotype of the Birmingham "racist" popularized by press and television, he said: "I told myself some time ago that we might as well get ready for changes in the South." But then he went on, giving a new turn to his thought: "Just the same I don't understand these Negroes. Why do they want to lose the good will of the white man? Why do they insist on pushing so hard?"

And so my friend added his word to what Dabbs has called the "wide outcry among Southern whites about the loss of peace and understanding between themselves and the Negroes." You hear it everywhere. David Lawrence, the Washington columnist, not long ago gave over half his space to the plaint of an Atlanta woman: a "black face" is no longer the face of a friend, but "the face of a stranger." From Montgomery, following the Negroes' boycott of the segregated bus system, Dan Wakefield reports: "Judging from the whites I talked with recently in Montgomery, the successful boycott did not increase their respect for the Negroes who carried it out, but, rather, increased the mistrust and hatred of them." [2]

This mistrust is not limited to whites. The Negro sit-in demonstrators were so far from reposing confidence in Nashville's whites that they didn't even tell the white

leaders of the liberal, "do-good" category what was about
to take place. In another city, both whites and Negroes
agreed on the need for lunch-counter desegregation. But
each group apparently met separately. When outsiders
asked Negro leaders what they thought of the white
business leaders' plans for desegregation, the Negroes
had to say they had never heard about them. Thus a kind
of psychic separation between races occurs even in the
midst of efforts to remove the barriers of law and custom.
Thus there seems to be growing, as Francis Pickens Miller
has pointed out, a new, more ominous kind of segregation "of the mind and spirit, ... consciously practiced by
members of both races against each other."

But it is the white people of the South who make more
of this "breakdown of communication." Why? We already
have the answer. Genuine communication between men
does not take place until the parties stand before each
other as full-fledged human beings. When one of the
parties is kept as an adjunct or mere extension of the will
of the other, there is no communication, but only a
swallowing of the lesser by the greater. Let us recall, from
Chapter 3, the wisdom of Roger Mehl: "The primary
condition for communication is respect for the otherness
of the other." White men have tended to regard *benevolence* as their sole obligation to the Negro. But between
adults there is another obligation: neither love nor mercy
nor benevolence, however well-meant, can stand in lieu
of recognizing the recipient as possessing independent,
mature selfhood.

This is the whole point of the breakdown in communication in the South. The Negro has grown up. He is not going to be treated as a child any more. He is not going to accept the white man's benevolence in preference to asserting his manhood. To embrace peace and harmony before the manhood has been won means only a perpetuation of the status of childhood. That is why the Negroes aren't crying about the estrangement between the races. As Dabbs comments:

The Negroes . . . don't feel too keenly the ending of a peace that had been forced upon them. And it is being ended mainly because the Negroes don't care any longer to be loved by the whites. This naturally makes the whites angry, and they organize citizens' councils to make the Negroes let them love them again. . . . This is where you come out if you try to substitute love for justice.[3]

Numerous whites in the South fail to see this point. They continue to think that doing the Negro favors ought to pacify him. They continue to think that sitting the Negro down and "talking" to him will relieve him of his ambitions. But in the nature of the case there can be no genuine "talking" until the Negro is able to take part as himself instead of as an inferior from whom advance agreement is expected. In Clarenden County, South Carolina, one of the counties where the original school desegregation suits were entered, white leaders attempted a biracial meeting to talk out the issues. A white minister later described to John Bartlow Martin what happened: "The Nigras didn't have a lot to say. . . . They were afraid to say anything." A white banker set out to hand down his formula for racial harmony ("I told them they can make us close the schools, but they can't make us mix," etc.). Assent was obviously expected of the Negroes. And to get the meeting over with, that is what they gave. They bobbed their heads in time with the banker's dicta, but few showed up for the second meeting, and after that, no more were held.[4]

Such "communication," of course, is not much more than the white man's latest device for having his way with the Negro. On this showing, the breakdown in communication is not a sign of worse relations between the races, but a sign that there are from now on going to be independent parties in the South to *have* communication. To the objection that the Negro was making more progress before he chose to invoke this era of estrangement, the record itself is an adequate answer: it is dubious that the Negro has ever accomplished more in any decade since 1865 than in the one beginning in 1954, the year communication began to break down. And if it is argued that this objective progress since 1954 has come at the expense of "the good relations between the races" which formerly prevailed, we only have to point again to what those so-called "good relations" actually were: white superiority and benevolence, Negro inferiority and acquiescence. Now the Negroes are asking, without knowing it always, for a more biblical basis of good relations: justice as well as love; justice, in fact, as a sign of love.

A Flaw in Negro Thinking

One of the ironies in the struggle is that the "new Negroes" of the nonviolent movement commit the same error, formally speaking, as the segregationists, for they have their own form of the ethical dictum that "love" leads the way, and "justice" follows after. I make a point of it because, in my opinion, the Bible and most of the great theologians of Christendom see it the other way around: the view I shall defend holds that you have to have just arrangements, by law and other forms of pressure, as part of the community framework, whether you have love or not; and that love builds upon, and transforms, these external arrangements into something better.

The segregationist, as we have seen, classically insists on doing the Negro benevolences and favors, bestowing "friendship" on him in lieu of giving him his full rights. The Mississippi planter will not let his Negro tenants starve, though he doesn't want them to vote. The Georgia businessman will give generously to buy football uniforms for the Negro high school, but he isn't willing to have Negroes in the other high school. And so on.

"After the Negro earns his status," you very often hear the segregationists argue, "then it's time to start talking about justice." In the meantime he should take the white man's word for it that he "loves" the Negro.

In terms of structure, this is not so far from the sit-in demonstrators, and their views on theology. Of course, justice is the big, main object for the new Negroes. That in itself is a difference from the segregationists, whose big, main object is to defer justice for the Negro as long as possible. And yet, the nonviolent demonstrators make quite a point of the fact that they are going to "love" the white man as a way of getting "justice."

"As you press on for justice," said Martin Luther King in one of his sermons preached in Montgomery, "be sure to move with dignity and discipline, *using only the weapon of love*" (my italics). In an address to the Southern Christian Leadership Conference in Nashville not long ago, he asserted: "It is possible to stand up every day against segregation and to love the segregationist."

King borrows this idea, in part, from India's Mohandas K. Gandhi, whose nonviolent method of *satyagraha*, or "insistence on truth," had in turn been inspired partly by the "love ethic" of Jesus. As King explains it:

Love for Gandhi was a potent instrument for social and collective transformation. It was in this Gandhian emphasis on love and nonviolence that I discovered the method for social reform that I had been seeking for so many months.[5]

King's followers have tried to take his views seriously. They wore buttons imprinted with the slogan "Father, Forgive Them" when King was arrested in Montgomery. In Nashville, they gave out mimeographed sheets during the lunch-counter demonstrations saying that the protesters were only applying the Gospel of Love, working for reconciliation, and carrying out a method which "makes the kingdom of God possible *now* rather than a future kind of hope."

The mistake the Negroes have made here, I think, is partly semantic. They assume that not-using-physical-violence is a suitable referent of the verb "to love." If they see, then they do not admit, that the choice of weapons, violent or nonviolent, has little to do with the inner state of the user of the weapons. He may or may not love his opponent.

But the mistake is more theological than semantic. It is a failure to take the biblical description of man's frailty seriously to insist that we can go about massively loving those who oppress us. All men, even the "new Negroes," are too involved in their own anxieties and fears and pride and impulses to be so purely and continually other-centered. If the theological wisdom of the past generation has taught us anything, it is that the human self is mightily capable of self-deception—most of all when it pretends to unmixed piety or disinterested love of one's enemies. To be sure, the Christian believes that God's love for him gives him freedom to love others, even those who do him wrongly. But this love of ours for others is never pure and unmixed, never up to the level of God's love for us, never out of the danger of being cloyed with self-interest or the simple (and sinful) spirit of retribution.

What the sit-in theology needs is fuller awareness that the deepest hatreds can be communicated by nonviolent means, just as the deepest love can, depending on the circumstances, and that the breakdown of communication in the South now, and the mutual antipathy (and hence lack of love) is real on both sides, white and Negro. It is not a question of uniformly loving Negroes who suffer in order to elicit justice from uniformly unloving whites: as neat as that sounds, it is theologically but a description of pride on the part of the Negroes who claim such virtue. The situation is rather, I am afraid, a

case of Negroes, at once loving and unloving, who rightly
and wisely use pressure to exact justice of whites—also
both loving and unloving. "The educated Negro in the
South," Hodding Carter claims, after making a study,
"dislikes the Southern white man en masse as never before in our history." [6] King himself has begun to grasp
this sober truth, I think, and to see that the strength of
the nonviolent movement does not lie in any superhuman
ability to love one's enemies, but rather in its peculiar
ability to channel discontent, dislike, anger, impatience
into quiet, effective outlets: the outlets of nonviolence.
Though nonviolence is "more successful" than violence,
he points out, yet "it does not require" that its participants "abandon their discontent." [7]

Should Justice Be Coerced?

Let us return for a moment to the steel-company employee from Birmingham. "We'd be a darn sight more
willing to see the Negro get his rights," he grumbled,
"if we weren't being pushed into it." The pushers he had
in mind were (1) the Federal government; (2) Northern
moralists; (3) the Negroes themselves, especially the
Negro collegians.

The real question before us has been confused by all
sides, but especially by white Southerners. Arching his
back against pressure, legal or moral, this Southerner is
still likely to insist, even today, that he will do more for
the Negro if he is let alone. He will tell you the white
South was going to free the slaves sooner or later, anyway, and that the use of Federal arms was simply a mis-

taken way of forcing things that in various ways defeated its own purpose. He will tell you that he "loves the Nigra" today, was just about ready to let him vote, or give him better schools, or find him better jobs, when all this Federal power and this outside agitation and these "uppity Nigras" themselves came along "and set progress back fifty years."

Let's examine this extravagant claim. Would the Southerner have *voluntarily* abandoned public-school segregation, for example, in the foreseeable future without pressure from the courts and the more militant Negroes themselves? The very compliance of Southerners with court orders has ordinarily been accompanied by damaging admissions to the contrary. When twenty-one Negroes entered public schools at Norfolk and Arlington, the Richmond *News-Leader,* no rabble-rousing journal, sadly observed: "We do not see this sociological venture as good, but as a positive evil.... Virginia submits only in recognition of superior force." The point of this editorial, patently, is not that "we would have done it willingly if you hadn't forced us"; the point, rather, is to the effect that "we wouldn't do it at all, if we weren't being made to." Even the moderates take much the same line, it might be noted. To insist, under the rubric of "law and order," that "we must do this because the courts now require it" is but a graceful way, for some, of saying: "We probably wouldn't do it unless the courts *did* require it."

A conservative Supreme Court, from shortly after Reconstruction until about 1935, usually interpreted the Constitution in favor of Southerners. Especially did the

Court give the South a great deal of leeway where the Fourteenth Amendment, with its guarantees of equality, was concerned. Did Southerners use this freedom, this chance at voluntary action, to work out for themselves the problems connected with the Negro's struggle for equality? Robert J. Harris, a Southern political scientist who has studied this two-generation span of relative freedom from Federal interference, concludes:

It is melancholy to record that the southern states, instead of using their newly restored powers over race relations to bring about a gradual improvement of the legal, political, and economic status of Negroes, used them in a discriminatory and oppressive manner, with a view to keeping the colored race in a low, servile, and cringing status. . . . [8]

"The plain fact," argues William Peters, "is that nearly every evidence of significant progress on the long road toward Negro equality of opportunity in the North as well as the South has come about, directly or indirectly, as a result of legal coercion or the threat of it." As long ago as 1932, Reinhold Niebuhr put the matter bluntly: "The Negro will never win his full rights in society merely by trusting in the fairness and sense of justice of the white man." Niebuhr, in a remarkable piece of prophecy of the future, suggested that the Negro avoid violence but that he nevertheless use "economic and political pressure . . . which will . . . exert coercion upon the white man's life." [9]

The segregationist, however, still has another line of defense: "You can't legislate good race relations." Or in the pious phrase of the Methodist Layman's Union of Alabama, the Negro cannot hope "to win by force of law what only mutual good will and respect can make permanent." And the Southerner is right on this point, in an important sense. No one, indeed, can secure neighborliness by coercion. Yet this line of thought is finally dishonest, for it ignores the fact that the worst effects of injustice *can* be minimized by pressure and legislation. The Constitutional amendment allowing women to vote didn't, by any means, eliminate the prejudice of thousands of Americans against "women in politics." But this piece of legal pressure did relieve *external discrimination*, at the ballot box, against women; and it was followed, of course, by a change of attitude also, for women shortly were generally accepted as voters and participants in the democratic process.

The same thing happened when the armed forces were integrated racially. Government directives requiring that white and Negro soldiers live, eat, and train together didn't change anybody's attitude. But many Southerners, led into close contact with the Negro through this pressure, learned to see him for the first time as a man endowed with rights and as a being capable of fellowship. In short, the silliness of segregation became obvious.

But there are better arguments for the use of pressure than these practical ones. The Scriptures themselves think of God as not only "loving," but also as concerned, at a minimum, to require "justice." The prophet Amos is doubtless anxious for his fellow Jews to love each other. But he does not think fair play has to wait for the day

when this ideal comes to reality. In the meantime, Amos
is certain, God judges severely those princes of Israel
"who oppress the poor, who crush the needy." Amos calls
for justice in the sternest tones:

> The Lord God has sworn by his holiness
> > that, behold, the days are coming upon you,
> when they shall take you away with hooks,
> > even the last of you with fishhooks.
> . . . Because you trample upon the poor
> > and take from him exactions of wheat. . . .[10]

From the ancient Church's Augustine to the twentieth
century's Reinhold Niebuhr, Christian theology has made
a place for the justice of God as a kind of forerunner
of the full will of God. Because God judges the unrighteous
severely, said John Calvin in a classic sixteenth-century
statement, the justice of God both reveals to men their
lack of love and forces them to be restrained in public
pending a change of heart. Though it indeed makes no
one righteous or loving to conform externally to the "Law
of God," says Calvin, "Nevertheless, this forced and ex-
torted righteousness is necessary for the good of society,
its peace being secured by a provision but for which all
things would be thrown into tumult and confusion."

Those who have gone through a change of heart reli-
giously, Calvin believed, realize by experience that the
Law of God "had the effect of keeping them in some
degree in the fear and reverence of God, till, being
regenerated by his Spirit, they began to love him from
the heart." Or as Jonathan Edwards, America's greatest
Calvinist, put it later: "We may conclude that those who

are actually redeemed by Christ, and have a true discovery of Christ made to their souls, have a discovery of God's terribleness and justice to prepare them for the discovery of his love and mercy." [11]

Modern students of Christian ethics have come to analogous conclusions, though usually with greater stress on the forces of justice as they bear upon social evils. To be sure, many are likely to insist, with Paul Ramsey, that "the Bible knows nothing, or little, of any conflict between justice and love." And yet, in the affairs of men, they readily concede a kind of priority for justice, given the sinful state of society. If love is "the internal basis and meaning of natural justice," then justice is the external condition for love, "the promise and possibility of closer meeting." According to Reinhold Niebuhr, we may well have to start with the securing of justice if we are to be able to love our neighbors at all: "It is fairly clear that a religion which holds love to be the final law of life stultifies itself if it does not support equal justice as a political and economic approximation of the ideal of love." [12]

Enforced justice, then, "puts the visible sin of man under judgment and restraint" (Kyle Haselden); it is the way love goes about creating conditions for its entrance into a sinful world.

It remains to be seen whether such instruments as the Federal courts, the Attorney General's operations, the pressures of the nonviolent movement, and so on, are actually to be identified with the "Law of God," and with the "justice" which theologians see as part of the

"Word of God," the forerunner to the spread of love and neighborliness among men. Indeed, it is clear that these forces are not to be taken for the way God himself would go about solving our problems if he were in the habit of supplying us with detailed blueprints for righteousness. And yet, seeing that God does not leave himself without a witness, and expresses his will in the crucial times, and even uses secular forces as instruments of his will, we must insist that these pressures undoubtedly do, in some fashion, represent the judgment of God upon the failure of twentieth-century Americans to live together freely and responsibly. We must not finally identify legal decisions and government directives with the Word of God. Nor is the nonviolent movement that perfect embodiment of "higher law" that its sponsors seem to imagine it is.[13] God's Word is not, in the last analysis, a piece of legislation or pressure at all, but an invitation to trust and neighborliness. Still, God is able to use all these forces, however sinful and inadequate they may be in themselves. If court rulings and sit-in pressures are not the best possible steps in the right direction, just the same they are more nearly that than anything the Citizens' Councils have suggested. God will judge us all, in the end, and insist that we replace compelled justice with the heartfelt impulse to neighborliness. In the meantime, we are not to spurn the value of compelled justice.

The Next Step

In *Uncle Tom's Cabin*, Mrs. Stowe hit upon a neat solution for the problem of race relations. Though she argued that the freed Negro was entitled to full status as a citizen, she actually suggests that the Negro might prefer being sent back to Africa. In a sense we can say that the question of *justice*—emancipation of the slaves itself—was the only important issue to her. She had the advantage, for this reason, of being able to talk about a clean-cut solution. She did not go on to the fearfully complex question of how whites and Negroes might begin living together.

If we insisted, in the preceding section, that justice must be assured before there can be real communication between the races, we must now go on to insist, just as firmly, on the completing truth: *justice alone is never enough.* It never is enough, either to carry out the purposes of God, or even to create a sound social order. Justice, alone, is a denial of God's mercy. For justice, at most, is but a forerunner of neighborliness; it is but a setting of outer conditions for the inner growth of charity.

Let us recall one reason for the failure, as a Christian movement, of the Social Gospel. It tended to stop with the winning of bare justice. It was content to see the working man economically bettered. It did not press on vigorously enough to see the working man re-enrolled in the Church, and so it did not, in the long run, hold up the inner life of Christian community as the goal of economic betterment. Today, I fear, the desegregation movement is in peril of the same fate. It has insisted almost single-mindedly on the securing of objective, outward justice for the Negro. But it has not really put too much thought on the equally important task of asking

how the Negro and Southern white may become genuine
neighbors.

The problem before us, then, is the most serious of all
theological tasks. It is to find a way of co-operating with
the Word of God all the way instead of just partly. It is
to find a way of building love upon the hard-won estab-
lishment of equality. If the solution now being painfully
hammered out in step after step of desegregation is to
be permanent and healthful, then it must go to these
internal and individual questions as well as the external
and social ones. It is not enough to "limit the effects of
prejudice through education and legislation." Such progress may relieve discrimination but does not cure prejudice "in the white man or, for that matter, in the Negro"
(Kyle Haselden). Unlike Mrs. Stowe, we have to face
the fact that two races must become full equals and begin
to live together. It is already the Number One problem
in a real sense, for, as we have seen, the legal barriers
to desegregation are tumbling. The time is upon us,
especially upon the Church, to say how we believe
Southerners—white and Negro—may enter upon the era
"beyond desegregation," when rough justice may be available, but neighborliness has not yet been realized.

I would offer the following suggestions for going about
it:

• *The meaning of what is required of us should be
understood in its theological dimensions.* So far, we have
attempted to set both segregation and desegregation into
perspective by theological inquiry. The former we saw

as a religion and theology of its own built on the theological phenomenon of pride. The latter, with its pressures toward justice, we have reduced to size by calling it only a preliminary part of the Word of God which ranks neighborliness as a higher good than justice. Now, it remains to be suggested that the meaning of life itself in the South is best understood, also, as a theological reality: as life lived under the will of God for man.

And here, just because we are sticking to a theological analysis, we come to a point, at last, where we can fully endorse one of the axioms of the conventional Southerner, namely, that "living together" is a voluntary matter. It is indeed that. It is indeed a matter for private decision. It cannot be legislated. It cannot be forced. Public equality may be amenable to compulsive measures, but neighborliness is built on voluntary, freely chosen associations. We insist that this is so for theological reasons. God never *forces* anyone to enter into fellowship either with him or with other men. The Word of God may confront a man with his pride and selfishness for remaining apart, but only the man himself may respond to God's invitation to move through these barriers.

Some of my worst hours have been spent at church camps and other Christian places where it was assumed that everyone there *had* to be equally friends. So all twenty of us on the staff at one camp went to the movies together one night. Attempts to strike up more particular friendships on the basis of mutual interests were constantly foundering on the fear that it would not be Christian treatment of the others. I prefer Augustine to this group-happy theology. All men are to be loved equally, he concedes. But you cannot love all at once. So you are to pay special regard to those who "by the accidents of time, or place, or circumstance, are brought into closer connection with you." That is good Christian thinking, and good Southern thinking.

To be specific, I think we must conclude that no human being can insist, as if it were still a matter of justice, upon the *right* to fellowship. Love can be offered, but not forced. On the other hand, we must insist that the white man who refuses to cross the racial line with his neighborliness know where he stands, theologically speaking. He is free in the sense that he can do as he pleases; yet it is also true that he is not free of the "unrepentant Kingdom" so long as his acceptance of desegregation is at the purely public or compulsory level. Going along with measures of justice does not reach the real point of the matter, which is that the Negro, as a son of God, has more than a legal standing alongside other men. No Christian can tell another just how he is to honor the great commandment to love his neighbor. But the Church has a duty to preach the commandment of love itself as a fulfillment of all external, compulsory commandments which deal in forced togetherness.

Although the Southerner has been loudest of all in his insistence upon "voluntary association," he is perhaps the furthest of all from taking it seriously in the theological sense. For it means not that he should be free of legal pressures to desegregate, but rather that he is still very much on the spot, as a Christian, after legal desegregation is complete. (We must say more about this problem below, when we consider the Church's responsibilities, in the present crisis, to teach the meaning of neighborliness.)

• *Implementing the meaning of neighborliness in the South can best be performed by Southerners.* I do not say that Southerners alone should administer justice to the Negro. Like any other group of men, we are too caught up in self-interest; we need outside pressure, as much as I regret it, even from itinerant Northern moralists. But as for proceeding with our further responsibilities "beyond desegregation," that is very much a different matter.

Let us attempt to profit by experience and history. Along with the military troops and carpetbaggers, Reconstruction brought a flood of Northern parsons and missionaries into the South. I do not wish to discount the good these visiting divines did, especially for the Negro (such institutions as Fisk University are a result of the work of Northern Christians following the Civil War). But I would suggest that a great deal of this work among white Southerners was vitiated—by self-righteousness, by not knowing how to act on good intentions, by handling the inward problem of "conversion" in the same way as the outward problem of "justice."

It was the sincere conviction of northern church members that the southern churches had become so depraved that only with the help of northern missionaries was there any hope of their being cleansed. To such a task the North had been summoned by God; His agents were the churches and the radical elements of the Republican party.... Southern churchmen, however, ... greeted the invaders with bitter invective and scorn.[14]

Perhaps through the abrasion of failure, the Northerners soon lost interest in converting the whites of the South and settled down to the more pedestrian task of educating the Negro. Our interest in this subject is more than antiquarian. The same situation is presented again, in the aftermath of desegregation. Hence grave dangers are present. Northerners do have considerable business in the South where the injustice of racial laws and customs is at stake. But when it becomes a question of the Southerner's failure, beyond desegregation, to *love* the Negro, the matter is not so simple. On this part of the problem, the Northerner would do well to attend to his own shortcomings, for he, too, in his own way, has failed to love the Negro. Both the impulse to love and the mandate to seek justice can be existential questions, matters of personal response to the invitation of God. But love, unlike justice, cannot ever be humanly enjoined.

There is another, more important reason for insisting that the Southerner must work out his own salvation, in fear and trembling, at the level of neighborliness. He cannot afford to let the North, or the Federal judiciary, or the "new Negro" be his conscience for him. He must, for salvation, be in possession of his own faculties for deciding between good and evil. It is one thing to say he can be made a party to justice by outside restraints and pressure. It is another question, how he can be made whole; he must take on this fearful challenge for himself.

Though I suspect this particular line of reasoning is not what lies behind the remark of Dwight L. Dumond, it is still in order here:

> Emancipation did not come from conviction of sin on the part of the slaveholders; and, in the course of time, an unregenerate people ... crushed the reborn spirit of freedom, and reduced the Negro again to a refined form of slavery commonly called second class citizenship.[15]

Finally, I suggest, the South must work out its own way to neighborliness with the Negro (always assuming the prevenient operations of justice, of course) because it, more than any other region of the country, knows what neighborliness is. With its sense of *place, personalness, localness,* and *leisure,* no part of America is so well furnished to embrace the second great commandment, to love neighbor—if it did not lack one thing. This one thing is a change of heart and attitude. It is the responsibility of Southerners to try to transcend their existential block toward the Negro, preferably on the basis of Christian faith. If we can do it we can show forth the meaning of neighborliness in unparalleled fashion.

• *The Church, as Church, has a peculiar responsibility for advocating neighborliness beyond justice.* In Florida, the Grand Dragon of the Southern Knights of the Ku Klux Klan handed in his resignation, explaining: "I see no way to stop racial integration in the schools and it looks to me like the best thing to do is accept it. ... I cannot agree to go outside the law to maintain segregation. I cannot agree to such things as bombing and burning schools." [16] But Bill Hendrix was not yet done. Though he was for law and order, "I still say I am for segregation." He made it clear that he was merely moving back to a new line of defense. For now, he said, *he would continue his fight against integration through the church.*

One lesson to be drawn has to do with realism. Even a Grand Dragon of the Klan knows segregation in public places is done for. Only the "wooly-minded," said Ralph McGill, should miss the point now, after what Bill Hendrix did.

But another lesson is to be drawn, too. And this is that the center of the struggle is changing and a new phase of it is beginning. As segregation dies civically, it takes on new life behind the scenes, in places where men gather voluntarily. Most conspicuous of these places is the *Christian church.*

In the church Hendrix will find numerous coworkers in the cause of white supremacy. He will find people like those in the several Methodist Layman's Unions which propose to resist to the death, as one of them phrases it, any "intimate and familiar associations of the Negro and white races." He will find Calvinists like those of Columbus, Georgia, who got rid of their preacher with arguments before Presbytery to the effect that "No nigger will ever darken the door of the church," and "If a nigger comes, I go." [17] He will find Episcopal bishops who oppose the "new Negroes" and their quest for freedom, and he will find Baptists who cannot trust their own theological seminaries—they might give Martin Luther King a hearing.

On the other hand he will find Methodist bishops from the South who declare:

There is the contemporary South. Much of it is good and I am loyal to that good, but . . . its racial attitudes are sub-Christian, wrong, and a peril to this nation. . . . I am fully aware that if we ministers of today take the fully Christian attitude in this race issue, we will be criticized, perhaps in instances ostracized, and in the extreme situations we may even lose our jobs. But for myself I have settled the matter. Come what may, on this matter at least, I have decided to be Christian.[18]

He will find Catholic bishops in the South who say: "I am happy to take the responsibility for any evil which might result from different races worshipping God together. But I would be unwilling to take the responsibility of those who refuse to worship God with a person of another race." He will find Baptist ministers like the Rev. Paul Turner who, after being beaten by racists for escorting Negro children to school, preached the next Sunday: "There is no color line around the cross." He will be able, more than he suspects, to run upon Christian laymen like the one in a small Florida town who told me quietly at the post office one evening what he privately thought about segregation: "The whole thing is stupid and cruel."

But mostly he will find in the church those multitudes who have done or said little on the question.

Up to now, despite racists and foot-draggers, the Church has been able to acquit itself respectably enough on the issue of desegregation in public places. For the issue up to now has taken the form of a question of justice: shall the Negro have his civil and public rights? Or, alternatively and less boldly: shall law and order prevail in the land? When the question is put in these ways, the Church has been able either to take a stand—strong here, weak there—or else take refuge behind the stout armor of the secular agencies committed to justice. To put what I have just said less charitably, the Church has been able to get by even without displaying original leadership (except among Negroes), because it has been able, in effect, to rely on the leadership of the Federal Courts, major league baseball teams, Southern editors like Ralph McGill, college professors here and there, and various humanistic, do-gooder agencies.

From now on, the Church will be less able to avoid direct responsibility, for, inevitably, the issue before us is changing, away from relations between Negroes and whites defined legalistically or publicly, toward another area: the area of how men are to live with men. As the demand for objective justice is met, agencies which have justice as their highest concern will escort the Church no further across the battlefield. But the Church's concern is for more than objective justice; it is for fellowship, or realizing the commandment to make neighbors. Here the Church will have to rise to its challenge, or fail to be the Church. It will have to face the enemy without the protective convoy of the courts and other dreadnaughts that have borne so much of the brunt of the struggle so far.

What does this imply? As with the individual, it is

impossible to outline in advance a suitable blueprint or program by which the Church can enact the great commandment to foster the making of neighbors. We just cannot lay down a set of things for a congregation in such-and-such a town to do if it would advance neighborliness between white and Negro. The Church cannot coerce men into practicing fellowship, neither can it be coerced by men into artificial or forced groupings, which would amount only to a travesty of real fellowship. Here, too, we must say, the coming into reality of neighborliness, even for the congregation and church, is a matter that rests upon voluntary consent.

My personal belief, however, is that neighborliness as a congregational reality taken seriously means, at a minimum, the possibility of Negroes and whites worshiping together. I would insist that a congregation which lays down as a compulsory directive the exclusion of Christians, in principle, on account of color, has *not* taken hold, in a saving way, of the notion of neighborliness. I know what my friends in several small-town churches will say to this. "The Negroes don't want to come here and worship." That may be so, but the issue is not whether the Negroes want to come; it is whether they are welcome. To be realistic, however, perhaps we must look to some new form of gathering to supplement that found in the conventional local parish.

• *Only the Church, with the Gospel, has the full truth about what "men living together" really means.* We have already noticed mild pessimism among some ethicists who doubt that there are going to be any significant breaches of color and class lines in the institutional, local church as it presently exists. "The sharp edge of the Christian engagement with the modern world is not likely to be in the parish," says Peter L. Berger. "The most urgent tasks before us can be dealt with outside the institution and, ... outside the local congregation." [19] I believe this is a bit jaunty. I would agree that the business at hand, the making of neighbors, may have to be carried on across the color line by comparatively few Christians and usually in contexts somewhat removed from the Men's Bible Class. Yet there is more hope in this case-hardened, institutional church than we may think.

For one thing, we can still hear the Word of God in the local church, with all its crusty endorsements of the status quo. This is where most of us have, in fact, heard it. Moreover, those of us who seek to make some response to this Word in the field of race relations are under the strongest obligation to make that response in some kind of proximity to the local church, so that the implications may be seen by other Christians. This is the hard way of going about seeking new forms, but it is, in my opinion, the responsible way.

What, then, does the Church's gospel say to us, if we listen? It tells us that Christians cannot indefinitely live together purely on the basis of a legally defined relation. One man can't be a neighbor to another if the first insists that he is obligated to the second only to the degree that the letter of the law requires. On the other hand, everything beyond this point, for the Christian, is voluntary and unforced, regulated only by the mutual concern of men for each other. What this means to me is that I am free of every "legal requirement" in finding neighbors, just as the Christian faith tells me I am free of the law in every other part of my salvation.

I am still going to use good sense and ordinary judgment. I'm not planning to invite Negroes I don't know to come home with me. Doubtless I'm not going to take up a whole lot of time with anyone, of whatever skin color, who doesn't share at least some interests and tastes with me. To engage in forced-draft fellowship across color lines, as some professional liberals do, is no more than one more form of salvation by works. Neighborliness in the sense the church teaches is bound up with Christian liberty. On the other hand, the Negro graduate student in theology and his girl friend who came to dinner at our house are simply friends of mine. We have much in common. I can discuss Paul Tillich with him and a host of other subjects. But along with all that, I just like him, and that settles it. He is my friend and one of those neighbors available to me on whom I choose to place some attention.

What does the Church have to do with all this? It may sound, indeed, as if we were back on the subject of the individual again. My point is this: the Church is the main voice in our society, I believe, which can offer us sure guidance about what the word "neighbor" really means. As a Southerner, it has been the Christian gospel, and certainly not my cultural upbringing, which has given me this theology student as a friend. This gospel, with its word about what it is to have a neighbor, has freed me, I now see, from a vast amount of nonsense, just as it frees every believer from all kinds of moralistic book-keeping and superstition on all other points of salvation.

I have been told, through the Scriptures and the Church which teaches them, that God takes me in with-out setting any legal requirements down as an obstacle course between him and me. I know, by analogy, that God sets me free to seek friends wherever I may find them. I am sure of this, I have a certain conception of this freedom of friendship, because of the coming of Jesus Christ, who in the flesh has set out God's neighborly intentions toward me. I daresay then, that the Church, as the place where the Scriptures are read and taught, as the place where Jesus Christ is taken seriously, will have to be the definitive voice in our society now on what it means to go beyond justice to fellowship in the proper sense.

The Church has the basic responsibility, I believe, of *teaching* this freedom of men to be neighbors. (If it can't be done in church school, then it must be done in the personal conversation and activity of those who see the point and would redeem the institutional church.) I would vote for no compulsion or force at this level. I would eject no segregationists from the Church, for example, for that might set the precedent for ejecting other types of sinners, and so I might be the next to have to go. Anyway, the Church is designed in the first place to take in sinners, which means it has room for both segregationists and integrationists, for we are all that. I would go further. Antisegregationists, too, can be pretty unneighborly at times, whether they realize it or not, especially where their attitudes toward segregationists are concerned. Tolerance and understanding are both called for on the part of those who would recommend these traits to others.

Theologically, there is one other point. To love one's neighbor is not, after all, enough. To put it alternatively, failure to love one's neighbor is not, in itself, the deepest sin. The fundamental, and original, problem is always man's straying from God, his proud rebellion against his Creator. The Church, then, has to go to the root of the matter. It has to teach that pride against God is the basic raw material of sin, and that the opposite of pride, humility, is the trait of every man who has turned back toward God. It is necessarily a double kind of humility: first, toward God; second, toward men. It is this fundamental change of heart toward God which really answers, at bottom, to the evils of "racial pride."

If the Church teaches this truth, we shall at last be able to see the preliminary question of justice itself in a different light. We shall see that the human habit of self-elevation may disfigure justice when the latter is sought as an end in itself. At many a small-town bus station in the South, the Negro is now free to use all the facilities. So he stands in the cafeteria line to buy a cup of coffee; this is justice. But is it? The quality of the justice done him is bled off by the contempt of the waitress and white customers. The Negro fails at this point, too. In Washington a band of Negro teen-agers severely beat a bus driver while Negro passengers sat and watched, making no effort to assist him. Both the beating and the failure to stop it were examples of ways the Negro uses his newfound freedom not to seek the white man's friendship, but to extend him hostility. Unless transformed by humility, human self-interest always has a way of twisting around the very conception of fair play so that justice itself falls far short of a humane quality. The Church, then, must finally insist that even the legal rights of men are in danger when men have not swallowed their pride.

I know what kind of reception these ideas are likely to meet. But the Church has faced massive resistance before. There was the remnant of the Old Testament, the tiny early Christian church of the catacombs, the outmanned and outvoted Luther at Leipzig and Worms, the voice of the few who carried on the Social Gospel, and so on. Today, we must frankly accept the possibility that the Church, as we know it, may fail. It may well be that God will have to use voices outside the Church to teach neighborliness, as well as justice. We have to face the possibility that Ralph McGill has described:

Every minister with any shred of awareness sees that, just as the racial issue is the greatest political issue before the world today, so it is for Christianity. If the first great commandment of Jesus, and the second which is "like unto it," have no validity in the minds of church members, then the churches are finished, or eventually will be.[20]

Fortunately, hope in the midst of forbidding situations is part of what the Church teaches.

• *There is no final historical solution to the problem of race relations, for every victory leads to a new challenge.* One December day in 1955, two thousand Georgia Tech students marched on the Governor's mansion in Atlanta. They were mad. They were youths with a cause. A religious cause? No. An ethical cause? No. A civic cause, perhaps? Not particularly. Theirs was, rather, an athletic cause. Governor Griffin had threatened to estop Tech's prize football team from playing in the Sugar Bowl. Tech's prospective opponent, Pittsburgh, it seems, had a reserve fullback named Bobby Grier. Bobby Grier was a Negro.

Marching down Peachtree Street toward the Capitol, the students displayed banners: "Griffin Sits on His Brains," "Talmadge Puppet Does It Again," "Grow Up, Griffin." Police failed to quell the mob. Finally, a representative of the governor appeared and shouted: "You'll play in the Sugar Bowl! Now go home!" And Tech did play in the Sugar Bowl.

Perhaps the furthest thing from the minds of most of the demonstrators was justice for the Negro. Yet it is just this sort of incident, multiplied by dozens over the past few years in the fields of education, athletics, and commerce, which has added forcefulness and weight to the pressure for justice. Tech's success in being allowed to play in an interracial football game only proved a vestibule to an eventual further problem. Georgians were broad-minded enough to hurdle this barrier. That only meant, in the economy of American history, that they would soon be asked to surmount larger barriers. And indeed, six painful years later, Georgia Tech was voluntarily admitting Negro students.

Even so, we may predict, Tech's challenges in the field of human relations have not been met by this latest advance, but only raised to a higher level.

This school's experience, completely secular in its dimensions, yet illustrates the Christian belief that God speaks in the events of history as well as in the sayings and deeds of the Church. He may speak through such critics of the organized church as the eccentric P. D. East, the Mississippi editor who publishes a weekly, the *Petal Paper*—chiefly, one gathers, not to make money, but to engage in devastating ridicule of white supremacists. "It was my opinion," said Editor East, reflecting on his strange journalism, "that to state facts straight about the wild beasts of the Magnolia Jungle was a complete waste of time. I held, and still do, that to poke fun at stupidity was more effective than hell-fire and brimstone preaching." [21]

Editor East is no doubt right. All the same, we must observe, his poking fun at the racists eventually will tend in the same direction as the Tech students' poking fun at Governor Griffin: it will lead to further questions. At some point in space and time someone else will come along the same road Editor East has bravely traveled and advance the case one more notch in intensity—by pushing through with persistence, for example, a school desegregation case and other tangible advances which at one time seemed impossible to contemplate for Mississippi.

Finally, out of the welter of all such secular tendencies, the Church itself will certainly have to face up to the old, familiar, heart-rending duty of saying that the problem is not exhausted at the level of "law and order," but that there are questions of charity-and-friendship-between-equals to be answered by Christians. The point is this: no struggle for *justice* is ever finally won. Every advance teaches us how we must yet do still more to be even fairer in our dealings. Much less, however, is a final victory in the quest for *neighborliness* ever achieved. Every advance on this level only convicts us anew of our own self-centeredness and impels us to seek fresh ways of living together as Christians. The most important thing the Church can do in this perennial crisis of "men living together" is to preach the hard truth about it: it makes new demands upon us every day, and it will not go away, on the one hand, or be solved in a sweep, on the other.

We often make a less excusable mistake. This is to think, as we encounter the more subtle problems of race relations, that we can leave the elementary ones behind. We get taken with the problem of Negroes entering white schools, and we forget that the "simpler" question of a decade or so ago—the Negro's right to the ballot—is not yet solved in large areas. I come from a small, surprisingly tolerant county in West Florida that for years has encouraged Negroes, with a yawn, to vote as they like. Yet just a few miles away there is another county which as late as 1961 had not allowed a solitary one of its 240 voting-age Negro residents to register.

On every imaginable civic and public front we can make indefinite progress in improving relations and arrangements. But in not a single case or place can we make an end of the whole problem by a once-for-all reform. The abolitionists imagined that freeing the slaves would win us the trophy of a clear-cut victory in human relations. Time showed that this act only opened up a Pandora's box of problems. We are now witnessing the slow death of the latest: public segregation. If by some chance it were completely eliminated, we would still not be able to call off our efforts, for a new manifestation of racial pride in some other form would surely break out to replace it.

A generation ago, Frank Tannenbaum in his wise book, *Darker Phases of the South*, listed several of the most serious problems our Southern region faced at the time. He had chapters on the Ku Klux Klan, bad labor conditions in mills, the cruelty of Southern prisons, the one-crop economy. Each of these problems still exists, despite repeated reforms; none exists in the same way it did before. His last chapter explored the most elusive problem of all: "the problem of Southern solutions." At the deepest level of man's confrontation with man, he suggests, there just is no objective, plannable, solution. The more things change, the more they stay the same:

A solution must be had. It must be had immediately, without delay, and it must be efficacious, final, and Utopian. Yet solutions are not available for real problems; all that may be arrived at is attenuation, relief, a resetting of the strain, a removal of some of the friction. All that may be asked for is a change in the relative position of some of the factors, for the problem, as a problem, remains in a new form—possibly under a new name—but it remains, and taxes the ingenuity of man to a greater subtlety and more finesse.[22]

Christian faith takes this point of view seriously, for it is based upon an authentic insight into human experience and history. And yet, after the Christian has acknowledged, because he and his fellows are human, that they will always have ever-more-subtle problems of "men living together" to face, he can also say: there is always hope, and enough real progress from one event to the next to give that hope a staying quality.

Summary

I have spent most of my space in this book on the South and its ways, for that has been my method of coming at the problem of men living together. I have condemned the South's pride (which is but a regional variant of what ails us all), championed its gift to be human and steady, and urged these latter attributes upon our national character. I have set out what I take to be the South's emerging change of heart toward the Negro—a change that is properly prompted by the strictures of justice, but which Christians hope will end in a more inward kind of neighborliness.

I have tried to suggest what kind of living-together is best for a country as diverse as ours: neither a formless merger of groups nor a cold stand-off among them, but warm encounter alive to divers kinds of experience, with no limits set on communication and fellowship. I have made much of the differences coined by experience and history between men, groups, regions. Yet I believe that we are one in Christ—in principle by creation and in actuality by the promise of redemption. There will always be discernible differences among men, in my estimation, as long as we are men in history, for only angels are not differentiated by their finitude. Time, place, and particular challenges mark us; our selfish choices disfigure us; and the judgment and grace meant for each of us in our pilgrimage even transform us according to our own special promise. Let us end on the promise of unity, and even on the present reality of unity. But it is a unity that builds upon, and bridges, the differences, for that is the only kind men know just yet. Still, if it is a Christian kind of unity, focused upon Christ, it is one in which the differences serve rather than block fellowship.

Notes for Chapter 5

1. *The Deep South Says "Never,"* copyright 1957, by John Bartlow Martin. Reprinted by permission of Ballantine Books, Inc.
2. *Revolt in the South* (New York: Grove Press, Inc.—Evergreen Target Books, 1960), p. 91.

3. *The Southern Heritage* (New York: Alfred A. Knopf, Inc., 1959), p. 241.

4. *The Deep South Says "Never"* (*op. cit.*), p. 65. I would not argue that love or benevolence is *never* genuine in the absence of justice. I would even insist that most of the benevolence shown by whites in the South toward the Negro has been both well-intentioned and helpful. Yet I would also hold that charity, in the present circumstances, is inevitably ambiguous in its effects and insufficient. *Cf.* Berger, *The Noise of Solemn Assemblies,* p. 144: ". . . in the American South the question may well be raised whether the efforts put into diaconal-type work among Negroes have not willy-nilly contributed to the maintenance of the segregation system. . . ." Berger suggests that a responsible approach includes both political action aimed at revising the social structure, and "the work of alleviation among individuals suffering under that structure."

5. Martin Luther King, *Stride Toward Freedom* (New York: Harper & Brothers, copyright 1958—Ballantine Books, 1958), p. 76.

6. Hodding Carter, "The Young Negro Is a New Negro," *The New York Times Magazine,* May 1, 1960, p. 118.

7. Martin Luther King, "The Time for Freedom Has Come," *The New York Times Magazine,* September 10, 1961, p. 118.

8. Robert J. Harris, *The Quest for Equality: The Constitution, Congress and the Supreme Court* (Baton Rouge: Louisiana State University Press, 1960), p. 108.

9. William Peters, *The Southern Temper* (New York: Doubleday & Co., Inc., 1959), p. 275; Reinhold Niebuhr, *Essays in Applied Christianity,* D. B. Robertson, ed. (New York: Meridian Books, 1959), p. 81.

10. Amos 4:2, 5:11 (RSV).

11. John Calvin, *Institutes*, II, 7, 10-11; Jonathan Edwards, *Select Works* (n.p.: Banner of Truth Trust, 1959), II, 68.

12. Paul Ramsey, *Basic Christian Ethics* (New York: Charles Scribner's Sons, 1950), p. 5; *Christian Ethics and the Sit-In* (New York: Association Press, 1961), p. 27; Reinhold Niebuhr, *An Interpretation of Christian Ethics* (New York: Meridian Books, 1958), p. 120.

13. The nonviolent movement would be strengthened, in my opinion, if its leaders were to lose some of their confidence in their ability to discern the precise lineaments of "the moral law of the universe." The question of what constitutes a "just" law as distinguished from an "unjust" one certainly deserves far more attention than it has received in this context. But the obligation to respect laws that may be "unjust" has probably not been explored sufficiently by either the nonviolent leaders or the neo-Confederates. A way could be found, I would suggest, by which the testing of a law by deliberate violation could be combined with greater over-all respect for the processes of orderly change (legislation and litigation) than was apparent, for example, in the "Freedom Rides" of 1961.

14. Clifton E. Olmstead, *History of Religion in the United States*, p. 40. Copyright 1960. Prentice-Hall, Inc., Englewood Cliffs, N.J. Reprinted by permission.

15. Dwight L. Dumond, "Democracy and Christian Ethics," *Journal of Negro History*, XLVI (January, 1961), 4-5.

16. Nashville Tennessean, January 6, 1961.

17. Ralph McGill, "The Agony of the Southern Minister," *The New York Times Magazine*, September 27, 1959, p. 16.

18. William T. Watkins, "Methodism's Present Task," *World Outlook*, August, 1960, Vol. L, No. 8, p. 378.

19. *The Noise of Solemn Assemblies* (New York: Doubleday & Co., Inc., 1961), p. 170.

20. Ralph McGill, "The Agony of the Southern Minister," *loc. cit.*, p. 59.
21. P. D. East, *The Magnolia Jungle: The Life, Times, and Education of a Southern Editor* (New York: Simon & Schuster, Inc., 1960), p. 183.
22. (New York: G. P. Putnam's Sons, 1924), p. 149.